A Garden Herbal

A GARDEN HERBAL

Anthony Gardiner

Special photography John Freeman

This edition first published in 1995 by
The Promotional Reprint Company Ltd,
Deacon House,
65 Old Church Street,
London SW3 5BS
exclusively for Chris Beckett in New Zealand and Chapters of Canada

ISBN 1 85648 322 3

Publishing Manager Casey Horton
Design Manager Ming Cheung
Designer Sean Bennett
Photography John Freeman

Printed and bound in Malaysia

Publisher's Note
Neither the publisher nor the author take any responsibility for the implementation of any recommendations, ideas or techniques
expressed and described in this book. Any use to which the recommendations, ideas and techniques are put is at the reader's sole
discretion and risk

CONTENTS

FOREWORD

As with many people my interest in herbs began with food; those wonderful flavours – basil, tarragon, thyme, coriander, chervil and so on. Herbs can be difficult to keep growing throughout the summer without going to seed, particularly the annual species, but many are a constant reminder of the Mediterranean, where the air is filled with their scent.

Herbs are one of our strongest links with the past, from ancient Egypt where records show that the Egyptians were using plant material as diverse as flowers, seeds, fruit, leaves and roots, as well as bark and wood, in medicine, perfumery and cooking. Herbs are the oldest form of medicine and therefore have been used and tested longer than anything else `- an early account of beneficial plants was written by the Chinese nearly five thousand years ago.

Culinary herbs have always been popular down the ages; it is interesting to ponder the way in which they have been used. Like everything else, the fashion of the day dictates which herbs are currently in favour. In 1699, for example, John Evelyn was recommending the use of pennyroyal in a savoury pudding, and as an 'excellent tea' when dried. Such uses would be unthinkable today. Equally, there was also rather a good recipe for young thistle, which would have been eaten in the same way as fresh asparagus tips, with melted butter.

After falling out of fashion in Victorian times, culinary herbs had something of a renaissance at the beginning of the century. In 1911, Frances Beardswell wrote: 'It is amusing to see the zest with which the cook or cooks will go out into the sweet fragrant garden while herbs are at the best and wander around it, gather a spring here, a spray there, and a leaf somewhere else, to bring it into the kitchen and put it into the soups or salads according to the needs of the day.'

Ornamental herb gardens are very much a part of gardening today. They can be formal, with box edging, or informal, with great clumps of frothy green leaves and scented flowers. From whichever interest you are approaching herbs, this book is a must. Written in a personal style, the author gives you the facts while remaining involved. This is not an encyclopedia of herbs, but an informed and detailed book about all aspects of herbs, starting with their history, through medicine, cosmetics, cookery and design - it is truly a garden herbal. His practical experience in growing and designing gardens with herbs will be particularly helpful to those who are trying to establish new gardens. The author will not only tell you what herbs you need and where to plant them, he will also give you a recipe for using them. Furthermore, you will find a useful chapter on maintenance which advises us not be impatient in the spring, but to allow those self-seeded seedlings time to germinate before one goes mad with a hoe on the first sunny day thatcomes along.

Over the past 25 years we have all become much more away of the importance that plants play in our well-being. This book will help spread the news.

Simon Hopkinson
Hollington Herb Garden 1995

INTRODUCTION

Now it behoves anyone, who desires to be a skilful herbalist, to be present when the plants first shoot out of the earth, when they are fully grown, and when they begin to fade. For he who is only present at the budding of the herb, cannot know it when full-grown, nor can he who hath examined a full-grown herb, recognise it when it has only just appeared above ground.

Dioscorides, AD 60

A love of a particular subject often begins with a book. With me, the love became a passion that led me to take up herb gardening as a career, and I have never been happier.

The book was bought for me years ago by my wife, when we were living in a bedsit in London, with no garden, not even a window sill to set a window box on. It was a simple herb book with descriptions of herb plants and their history, with very few illustrations. But it opened up a whole world of possibilities in my mind, and when we eventually bought a flat of our own with a tiny garden, I began to grow herbs myself.

The chance to grow herbs, even in the smallest of spaces, is a means into a better way of living. These infinitely useful and rewarding plants lead you into a world where you feel part of a process that has been going on for thousands of years. In Sir Thomas More's words, each herb has 'a dumb language', which imparts its history and survival to you. You somehow need to find out more.

This book is intended to be a guide to all aspects of herb cultivation and use, with a very personal approach. Some of the failures as well as some of the successes are here. I have concentrated on the most popular herbs, building up as strong a picture of them as I can from history and from modern research. The origins of herb wisdom and the manner in which herbs have become part of the culture of civilisations is all part of this picture.

Growing herbs and creating herb gardens, can be a very enjoyable experience. When I first began it was very much a case of trial and error. I hope to help you avoid some of the pitfalls, by showing some of the simple techniques necessary to success. The garden designs are based on gardens I have created for clients who have, themselves, been part of the creation process. All gardens eventually take on some of the personality of the owners. I have been very lucky with many of the people I have met and worked with. Their enthusiasm and interest in herbs have formed lasting friendships, and their gardens continue to change and develop.

There is an ancient yogic saying that, 'When the student is ready, the teacher appears'. When I first began to grow herbs I knew very little about herbal medicine. Taking time off to attend a course, I met Christopher Hedley, a member of the Institute of Medical Herbalists, who has an eminent scientific knowledge of herbs. Other 'teachers' then appeared as if by magic, and soon I had a network of helpful people encouraging me on my way. Among these friends, I have to include all those members of the Herb Trade Association, who have helped me and taken me into their confidence.

To write a complete book of herbs, you would need a truck to carry it around. There are so many herbs to consider in the world. But no book is complete without some culinary recipes. This, after all, is where most of us first experienced a herb – in cooking. A number of friends, professional and amateur, have helped me compile some new recipes, and my wife has included some of her most inventive ideas also. This is an area, I must confess, where my wife has complete sway.

We are only just beginning to rediscover some of the healing properties of herbs, and tapping into that vast resource of plant help. So I have included introductions to aromatherapy, homeopathic medicine and the wonderful world of Dr Bach's remedies. It is, I feel, essential to include the distaff side also; and so I have drawn attention to the hazardous - not lethal – aspects of herbs.

All together I hope this is a book to read by the fireside in the winter months, as well as a useful helpmate wherever you may be growing these wonderful plants.

Anthony Gardiner

A History of Herbs

The question 'What is a herb?' is often asked, and thanks to the ambiguous nature of herb plants, it is not the easiest to answer. The emperor Charlemagne, ruler of the Holy Roman Empire, decreed in AD 800 that all imperial lands should be planted with a list of 89 herbs. His adviser, an English monk called Alcuin, asked for a definition, to which Charlemagne replied that they were 'The friend of the physician and the praise of cooks.' This has proved to be a much quoted and worthy statement, but it does not cover all the other uses, aromatic, cosmetic, decorative, even poisonous, that herbs have.

A dictionary definition tends towards an overall botanical description: 'Any non-woody, seed-bearing plant which dies down to the ground after flowering.' This however fails to take into consideration plants such as the bay tree, rosemary, thyme and many other recognised culinary herbs. In the end, like so many things appertaining to herbs, the simplest approach is the most effective. Herbs are useful plants, and so the simple definition put forward by the Herb Society of America in the 1930s is probably the best to follow. The society stated that a herb is 'Any plant that may be used for pleasure, fragrance or physic.' This encapsulates most uses: eating is certainly pleasurable, as is the

Chives die down completely in the winter only to re-emerge in the spring, while woody-stemmed herbs such as thyme are evergreen.

sight and scent of many herbs. Fragrance includes pot-pourri, aromatherapy oils, nose-gays and old-fashioned strewing herbs. Physic includes medicinal uses, tisanes, soothing unguents and all revivers of the vital spirit. So I would happily accept this definition as including the entire 'holistic' nature of herb plants.

Early herbal manuscripts

The writings that influenced the golden age of the 16th and 17th century herbals arrived in Northern Europe by a very circuitous route.

The first serious moves in the scientific study of herbs were begun by a Greek pupil of Aristotle called Theophrastus (born 370 BC). His *Enquiry into Plants* listed over 500 species, with careful descriptions of each. In the main, these cover the plants of the Mediterranean region around Greece, but also include references to some species from Egypt.

In AD 600 an army physician who was serving under the armies of Nero prepared the definitive herbal of his age. It was called *Peri hulas iatrikes*, better known by its Latin name *De Materia Medica*. His name was Pedanius Dioscorides, and he came from Anazarba in Asia Minor. Each plant had a drawing with description attached, followed by medicinal information and adverse effects, if any. This document became the model for all future works up until the early 16th century. At about the same time Pliny the Elder produced his *Historia Naturalis* before dying while investigating the eruption of Vesuvius in AD 79.

There now began a tug of war between the Islamic and Christian faiths, each intent on the advance of learning. Manuscripts captured in the Islamic wars with the Byzantines were taken to the House of Wisdom in Baghdad. A vast amount of research was carried out, and teaching centres and pharmacies were set up as far afield as Spain and Salerno near Naples. The medical school in Salerno became a famous centre for the study of plant medicine, and there was reputed to be a library at Cordoba in the 10th century containing over 600,000 volumes on plants.

The Benedictine monasteries, established by St Benedict in the 5th century AD evolved from the teachings of St Anthony, a hermit garden from Fayum

in Egypt. In the 9th century the monks drew up an ideal plan for a monastery at St Gall, near Lake Constance, in Switzerland. At this time too, Walafrid Strabo (meaning Walafrid-the-Squint-eye), Abbot of Reichnau Abbey, also on Lake Constance, wrote his poem *Hortulus*, or *The Little Garden*. This delightful treatise, which went undiscovered for 600 years, sets out the manner in which the abbot created a herb garden from a wilderness. In the relative calm following the reign of Alfred the Great, two Anglo-Saxon herbals were written. They were: *The Leech Book of Bald*, and the *Lacnunga*.

Above: Shaped columns of myrtle frame an old stone seat in the tranquil surroundings of the garden at the Museum of Garden History in Lambeth, London. **Overleaf:** Sowerby's illustration of the herb meadowsweet, *Filipendula ulmaria* (referred to here as *Spiraea ulmaria*), published in 1826 and hand-coloured by the publishers.

The *Leech Book*, written on stout vellum and miraculously still in existence at the British Library, begins: 'Bald is the owner of this book which he ordered Cild to write. He was assisted by two Saxon doctors called Dun and Oxa, who supplied him with prescriptions. The book is a strange mixture of Christian ritual and superstition. Elves and goblins are much in evidence,

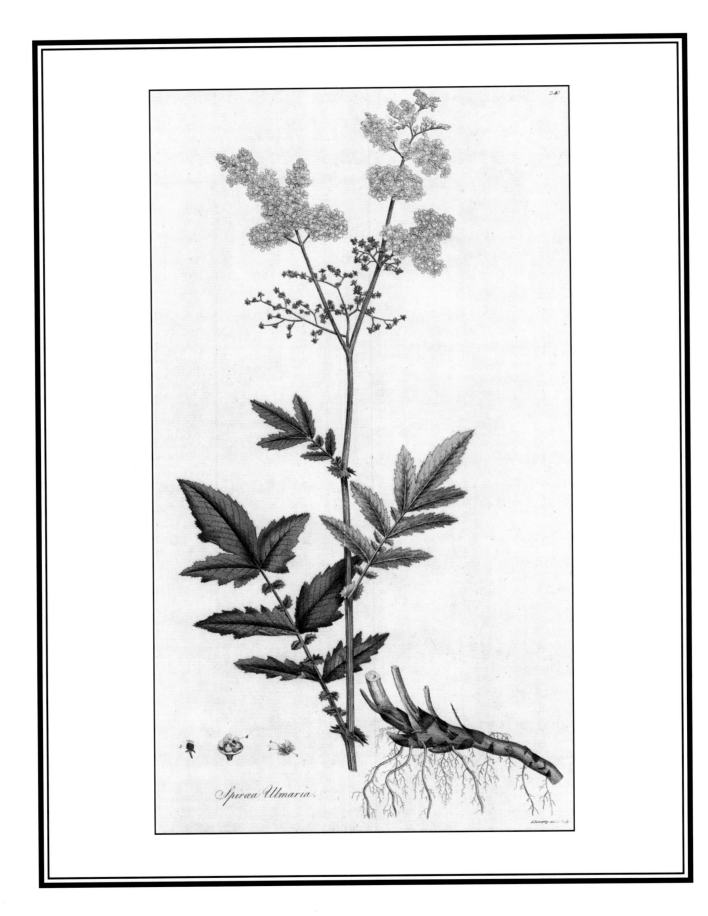

Spiræa Ulmaria.

Spiræa Ulmaria. Meadow-Sweet.

SPIRÆA *Lin. Gen. Pl.* Icosandria Pentagynia.

Cal. 5-fidus. *Petala* 5. *Capf.* polyfpermæ.

Raii Syn. Gen. 15. Herbæ semine nudo polyspermæ.

SPIRÆA *Ulmaria* foliis pinnatis: impari majore lobato, floribus cymofis. *Lin. Syft. Vegetab. p.* 393. *Sp. Pl. p.* 702. *Fl. Suec. n.* 440.

FILIPENDULA foliis pinnatis, acute ferratis, minimis intermiftis, extrema trilobata maxima. *Haller. hift. n.* 1135.

SPIRÆA *Ulmaria Scopoli Fl. Carn. n.* 603.

BARBA CAPRI floribus compactis. *Bauh. Pin.* 164.

ULMARIA *I. B.* III. 488.

REGINA PRATI *Ger. emac. p.* 1043.

ULMARIA vulgaris. *Parkinf.* 592. *Raii Syn. p.* 259. Meadow-Sweet. *Hudfon Fl. Angl. ed.* 2. *p.* 217. *Lightfoot Fl. Scot. p.* 259.

RADIX perennis, craffitie minimi digiti, obliqua, rubicunda, fibris plurimis ex fufco lutefcentibus defcendentibus inftructa.

ROOT perennial, the thicknefs of the little finger, oblique, reddifh, furnifhed with numerous fibres of a brownifh yellow colour, running deep into the earth.

CAULIS bi feu tripedalis et ultra, erectus, foliofus, angulatus, glaber, hinc inde rubicundus, plerumque fimplex.

STALK from two to three feet high or more, upright, leafy, angular, fmooth, here and there of a reddifh colour, for the moft part unbranched.

FOLIA alterna, petiolata, pinnata, 3-vel 5-juga: foliolis oppofitis, feffilibus, ovato-oblongis, fupra viridibus, glabris, lucidiufculis, lineatis, minutim venulofis, rugofis, fubtus nervofis, minutim tomentofis, cinereis, margine incifo-dentatis, undique ferratis, minutim ciliatis; terminatis foliolo majore, trifido-palmato.

LEAVES alternate, ftanding on foot-ftalks, pinnated, pinnæ from three to five pair, oppofite, feffile, ovato-oblong, above green, fmooth and fomewhat fhining, minutely veined, and wrinkled, the veins impreffed, beneath ribbed, covered with an afh-coloured downy fubftance, the edge jagged, ferrated, and finely edged with hairs, the terminal pinna large and deeply divided into three fegments.

PETIOLI fubtus convexi, fupra concavi; radicales triplo longiores.

LEAF-STALKS convex beneath, concave above, thofe of the radical leaves three times as long as the others.

STIPULÆ amplexicaules, acutæ, margine undique ferratæ, minutim ciliatæ; *partiales* in petiolo communi intra fingulum par pinnarum, fub oppofitæ, parvæ, inequales magnitudine, ovatæ, dentato-ferratæ, pariter fubtus tomentofæ.

STIPULÆ ftem-clafping, pointed, ferrated, and finely edged with hairs, the *partial* ones on the common foot-ftalk betwixt each pair of pinnæ, nearly oppofite, fmall, unequal in fize, ovate, indented or ferrated, and like the pinnæ downy underneath.

CORYMBUS terminalis, erectus, minutim pubefcens, pedunculatus, nudus, compofitus e cymis plurimis inæqualibus, intermedia feffili.

CORYMBUS terminal, upright, flightly pubefcent, ftalked, naked, compofed of feveral unequal cymæ, the intermediate one feffile.

CALYX: Perianthium monophyllum, fubcampanulatum, ad lentem pubefcens, pallidum, quinquefidum, laciniis ovatis, acutis, demum reflexis, *fig.* 1.

CALYX: a Perianthium of one leaf, fomewhat bell-fhaped, if magnified flightly downy, of a pale colour, divided into five fegments, which are ovate, pointed, and finally reflexed, *fig.* 1.

COROLLA: Petala quinque, albida, oblongo-rotundata, unguiculata, patentia, calyce duplo longiora, *fig.* 2.

COROLLA: five whitifh Petals, oblong, roundifh, clawed, fpreading twice the length of the calyx, *fig.* 2.

STAMINA: Filamenta viginti plura, filiformia, flavefcentia, longitudine corollæ, calyci inferta. Antheræ fubrotundæ, flavefcentes, *fig.* 3.

STAMINA: twenty Filaments or more, filiform, yellowifh, the length of the corolla, inferted into the calyx. Antheræ nearly round, and yellowifh, *fig.* 3.

PISTILLUM: Germina quinque, fex, five plura; Styli totidem, fuperne incraffati, reflexa; Stigmata capitata, *fig.* 4.

PISTILLUM: Germina five, fix, or more; Styles as many, thickened above and turned back; Stigmata forming little heads, *fig.* 4.

PERICARPIUM: Capfulæ plurimæ, fpiraliter contortæ, *fig.* 5.

SEED-VESSEL: Capfules feveral, twifted together fpirally, *fig.* 5.

The Meadow-Sweet has been juftly celebrated for its fragrance and beauty, the agreeable odour which the whole plant, but more particularly the flowers, diffufe, has recommended it for the purpofe of fcenting rooms, and purifying the air, by ftrewing it on the floors; it is faid not to affect the head like other perfumes: the leaves alfo, like thofe of Burnet, impart an agreeable flavour to wine and other liquors.

As an ornamental plant, it has long held a place in our gardens, not only in its wild ftate, but with variegated leaves and double flowers.

It puts in its claim alfo for medicinal virtues, which, however, do not appear to be of the moft powerful kind; the leaves are recommended as mildly aftringent, and ufeful in Dyfenteries; the flowers are faid to be antifpafmodic and diuretic: their pleafant fmell, in which their virtue refides, is foon diffipated by keeping.

It grows plentifully in wet meadows and by the fides of ponds and ditches, flowering from July to September.

Horfes and kine are faid to refufe it, fheep to eat it, and goats to be particularly fond of it; as it forms a great part of the pafturage in fome meadows, it is of confequence for the hufbandman more clearly to afcertain whether horfes and cows refufe the young foliage, and whether they reject the whole plant when made into hay.

We have frequently obferved fmall red tubercles on the leaves, which we have fuppofed to be occafioned by fome fpecies of Cynips.

Two women harvesting sage, in a print from the Herbal Health Handbook *Tacuinum Sanitatis*, dating possibly from the 15th century. Sage was reputed to be a herb that promoted long life. An old Arabian proverb says, 'How can a man die who has sage in his garden?'

and a number of remedies refer to being 'elf-shot', an affliction caused by the pricking of tiny arrows fired by aggrieved elves.

The *Lacnunga* is also steeped in magic and medicine and seems to concern itself a great deal with remedies for 'flying venom'. Meanwhile in Salerno a manual of preventative medicine was being written called *Regimen Sanitatis*. This was to lay the foundation for generations of medical herbalists. My favourite quotation from it sums up the philosophy of common sense:

> If you want to stay hale and healthy, stop worrying about trifles, have a light lunch, and do not strain too hard at stools. If there are no doctors around, do not worry: the best doctors are a happy mind and moderation in all things.

The first printed herbals

In 1476 William Caxton set up his first printing press in London. The first true herbal to come off the printing presses took another 50 years to appear. It was published by Richard Banckes, and although some scholars would suggest that it derived from an early medieval manuscript, it has all the hallmarks of an original work. In 1526, one year afterwards, there appeared *The Grete Herball*. This popular herbal was printed in Southwark by Peter Treveris, and used as its source a French herbal called *Le Grand Herbier*.

Both books are set out in the now-recognised style of the 'herbalis', or herb book. This has the names of plants with a description, and their properties and virtues. But the *Grete Herball* went a stage further, including advice on how to avoid being duped by quack apothecaries. The reader was being let into the hidden 'secrets' of the herbalist, and the way was prepared for self-medication.

Turner's herbal

In 1551 the publication of William Turner's *A New Herball* heralded the age of the classic herbals. From this work Turner gained the well-deserved title the Father of English Botany. It is, in every way, a completely original work.

Turner was born in Morpeth, Northumberland, during the reign of Henry VIII. Like many men to follow him he was what has since come to be recognised as a Renaissance man. Having studied divinity, he also became interested in medicine and plants, and was a physician and a botanist. His patron through university at Cambridge, and the man to whom he dedicated the second part of his herbal, was Thomas, Lord Wentworth. Turner says in his dedication: 'Wherefore I dedicate unto you this my little boke, desyring you to defende it against the envious evil speakers, which can alow nothing but that they do themselves.' This second part of the herbal was published abroad in Cologne, where Turner was living in exile during the reign of Queen Mary.

In 1558 at the accession of Elizabeth I Turner returned to England and was reinstated in the deanery of Wells. He was a powerful preacher, but prone to non-conformist behaviour, the most frowned upon by his superiors being the incident when he trained a dog to snatch the square cap from his bishop's head. Soon after this he left Wells and settled back in London at

Crutched Friars, where he had a notable garden. The third and final part of his great work was published in 1568, the year of his death, and dedicated to Queen Elizabeth in the firm belief that such a herb book was a right and meet gift for such a queen. The strength of his personality shines through at every page, whether he is eulogising about chamomile or chastising the superstitions surrounding the mandrake, and those who sought to capitalise on it. This was the first British scientific study of more than 230 of our native plants with exceptional woodcuts by Fuchs.

Gerard's Herbal

The fact that John Gerard used Dr. Priest's translation of Rembert Dodoen's work *Pemptades* for the botanical descriptions of the herbs, and without authority, doesn't spoil the enjoyment of this famous herbal one bit. Allowing for the justified criticism which this deliberate act of plagiarism has received, it is the personal observations and unique wit of Gerard that makes this one of the most enjoyable written works of the Elizabethan age.

John Gerard was born at Nantwich in Cheshire in 1545. He was a professional plantsman, and delighted in any rare or unusual introduction brought to him. He grew over 1000 plants in his garden in Fetter Lane, Holborn, where he prided himself particularly on his ability to grow even the most difficult of the foreign plants. 'These be strangers in England, yet I have them in my garden, where they flourish as in their natural place of growing.'

Gerard was well-respected by members of his profession, as is clear from his friendship with Jean Robin, keeper of the royal gardens in Paris. Of all the new vegetables being introduced into England at that time, he was one of the first to grow potatoes, which he refers to as the 'Virginia potato'. It has often been suggested that William Shakespeare was a friend of Gerard, as he lived close by to him, and the knowledge of herbs and wild flowers described in his later works in particular, undoubtedly share some of the folk quality that Gerard explained so keenly. Certainly Gerard's Elizabethan prose is romantic and cultured in its execution. A brief extract from his preface can vouch for that:

What greater delight is there than to behold the earth apparelled with plants as with a robe of embroidered works, set with Orient pearls and gar-

A 15th-century illustration showing a flowering mead enclosed by a wattle fence, with a rustic gardener receiving instructions from his master in the gathering of herbs. It is interesting to note the difference between the mead and the rather bland landscape in the background.

nished with great diversities of rare and costly jewels? ...The principal delight is in the mind, singularly enriched with the knowledge of these visible things, setting forth to us the invisible wisdome an admirable workmanship of almighty God.

The Herball was published in 1597 with over 1800 illustrations. Even these were the cause of some controversy. John Norton, the queen's printer, was given the loan of the woodcuts from a work called *Eicones* by Jacob Theodor and published in 1590. Gerard used them to illustrate his text, but made so many mistakes that the Flemish botanist, Mattias de l'Obel, was brought in to do the corrections. De l'Obel, no doubt out of professional zeal, claimed the need to do over a thousand alterations. Gerard settled the matter by declaring that de l'Obel had 'forgotten' the English language, and testified to its accuracy. De l'Obel never forgave Gerard for this insult to his professional pride, but it should be noted that it is John Gerard whose name we remember, and whose knowledge of plants was recognised as second to none. George Baker, a contemporary, wrote of a visit to Paris that Gerard 'was desirous to go abroad with some of our herbarists…when it came to the trial my French man did not know one to his fower.'

There does appear to be an enigmatic quality to Gerard's character. We know little of his life, but we glimpse a great deal of his charm, his humanity, his humour and his strength. His constant reference to plants that 'make men merry' points to a man you would just love to meet.

Parkinson's Herbal

In 1640, John Parkinson's *Theatrum Botanicum* was published. He was 73 years of age. In this lengthy work over 3800 plants are described. Parkinson's original intention was to name the book 'A Garden of Simples', which would have well described this treatise on all known medicinal plants. Somehow the *Theatrum Botanicum* failed to attract the popularity of one of his earlier works, *Paradisi in Sole – Paradisus Terrestis*. This was published in 1629 and his sense of humour is evident in the pun on his name, used in the title – 'Park in the sun'. He was well qualified to write a herbal on medicinal plants as he was apothecary to James I. He was great friends with John Tradescant the elder, and shared the confidence of Charles I and his wife Henrietta Maria to whom he dedicates his *Paradisus*. Following publication of the book he was appointed Botanicus Regis Primarius to Charles I.

Parkinson's garden was in Long Acre, and he delighted in visiting other famous gardens nearby, in particular, Master Ralph Tuggie's, where he claims he saw the 'most beautiful' gillyflower,' which he 'needes therefore call "Master Tuggies Princesse" '. In his classification of plants into 'Classes or Tribes' he refers to 'Venemous Sleepy and Hurtfull plants and their Counter Poysons', 'Hot and Succory like Herbs', and the 'Unordered Tribe': a group of 'stranglers that have either lost their rankes or were not placed in some of the foregoing orders that so I may preserve them from losse…'. I think we all have a group like that somewhere in our gardens.

Nicholas Culpeper

It is strange how out of adversity great things often transpire. When Nicholas Culpeper (1616-54) was at

In Effigiem Nicholai Culpeper Equitis

The shaddow of that Body heer you find
Which serves but as a case to hold his mind;
His Intellectuall part be pleas'd to looke
In lively lines described in the Booke.

Printed by Peter Cole
In Leaden-Hall

Nicholas Culpeper, astrologer and apothecary, who revolutionised health care for the poor people of Spitalfields and published *The English Physician Enlarged* (1653) as a guide to self-medication with herbs. This book is still one of the most popular herbals in the world.

Cambridge University studying Greek and Latin, he and his fiancée planned to elope. On her way to meet him her carriage was struck by lightning and she was killed. His academic life, in the comfortable, cloistered world of Cambridge, suddenly appeared a sham of luxury. Feeling desolate and embittered he left university and apprenticed himself to an apothecary in London, eventually setting up on his own among the desperately poor people of Spitalfields.

Having studied Latin he realised that it precluded everyone except the well-educated and the privileged classes. In 1649 he set about translating some of the learned works of the College of Physicians, and made them more accessible to the ordinary apothecaries. His first project was the *London Pharmacopoeia* (1649), in which he also pours contempt on those 'proud, insulting, domineering Doctors whose wits were born above five hundred years before themselves'. He was critical of high charges and the over-prescribing of drugs. Here was a man learned enough, and skilled enough to administer drugs with care and, above all, drugs to suit the poorest purse. In educating the common people about the virtues of English herbs he quite logically listed them by common name, and commented on the practice of the College of Physicians of using only Latin descriptions: 'It seems the College hold a strange opinion, that it would do an English man mischief to know what the herbs in his garden are good for.'

Nicholas Culpeper was a remarkable man. An apothecary who practised as a doctor, a puritan and a Parliamentarian. He appears to be a socialist ahead of his time and was greatly scorned and vilified by the establishment. Unmoved by this criticism, Culpeper played his trump card and published *The English Physician Enlarged* in 1653. This followed the tried and tested path of his own experience as a herbal practitioner with an added dimension, that of astrology and its influence on the plant world: 'He that would know the reason of the operation of the Herbs must look up as high as the stars.' This suggested 'quack' philosophy caused uproar among the conventional practitioners.

The English Physician was an immediate success and became a best seller. It still is. It has been published in more than 40 different editions. Maybe Culpeper hit on the right formula, maybe it was just a herbal for his time, but one thing is certain: Nicholas Culpeper's unselfish devotion to the craft of herbal medicine, and his obvious 'common touch' has guaranteed his name to live for many more years to come. He died young, from tuberculosis, in 1654 at the age of 38, leaving a wife, Anne, and seven children.

William Coles

Another theory taken up with zeal by William Coles in the 17th century was the doctrine of signatures. This idea was originally conceived by Theophrastus Bombast von Hohenheim (fortunately abbreviated to Paracelsus) nearly one hundred years earlier. He stated: 'I have oft-times declared, how by the outward shapes and qualities of things we may know their inward Vertues, which God hath put in them for the food of man.' These ideas were submerged for some time, probably as a result of the unpopularity of Paracelsus, but William Cole's two books *The Art of Simpling* (1656), and *Adam in Eden* (1657) argue in favour of 'signatures' in plants.

Coles attacked Culpeper's zodiac theories and accused him of being ignorant of 'the simples'. He then embraced the equally 'quack' theory of the doctrine of signatures as the new science and God-given guide to the medicinal virtues of herbs. He tells us that 'the mercy of god which is over all of his Workes Maketh Grasse to grow upon the Mountaines and Herbs for the use of Men and hath not onely stemped upon them (as upon every man) a distinct forme, but also given them particular signatures, whereby a Man may read even in legible Characters the Use of them.' He then goes on to illustrate heart trefoyle, hounds tongue (to be 'laid under the bottomes of ones feet' to stop them barking at you), and the walnut bearing resemblance to the brain. Other more obvious ones are pilewort, having roots like haemorrhoids, and lungwort, with its spotted leaves like the interior of the lungs. He searches about wildly to explain the lack of signatures on some plants, suggesting they therefore have no use. Sadly for Coles his arguments found few followers after his death and his doctrine was repudiated, slipping away into that obscure world of well-intentioned dreams.

Coles' book, *The Art of Simpling*, has chapters on the joys of gardening, which endear him much more to me because of his descriptions of the role a garden can play in healing the stress of everyday living. He writes:

> …there is no place more pleasant than a Garden … if a man be wearied with over-much study (for study is a weariness to the Fleash as Solomon by experience can tell you) there is no better place in the world to recreate himself than a Garden. There being no sence but may be delighted therein. If his sight be obfuscated and dull, as it may easily be, with continuall poring, there is no better way to relieve it, than to view the pleasant greennesse of Herbes … neither doe they only feed the Eyes but comfort the wearied Braine with fragrant smells. The Eares also have their recreation by the pleasant noise of the warbling notes which the chaunting birds accent forth from amongst the murmuring Leaves.

For this description of the 're-creation' of the senses I thank him most heartily. No hospice is without its garden, and I can think of no more comforting sight to see before that journey to another place and another garden.

With Coles' death, the Golden Age of Herbalism ended, and the New Science of the late 17th century hearalded a move towards orthodox medicine.

The Herb Garden:Style and Design

Deciding on the right style for your herb garden depends largely on your individual needs. The many uses herbs can be put to can make this choice for you. There are culinary, medicinal, traditional, formal, aromatic and even informal layouts. You can even go for a historical garden or plant to a theme, such as a paradise, Shakespearean or butterfly garden. The theme, or use, usually dictates the style, and from there you can develop your ideas and add other features.

Herb gardens are never dull. Often the considered opinion is, that because many of the plants have short flowering times and die down in the winter, then a herb garden is of limited interest. This merely shows lack of imagination. The fact that herb gardens have been cultivated since early times clearly demonstrates their versatility and durability.

Not everyone has a garden, but many flat-dwellers have either a balcony or a window sill. Very small gardens often have paved areas for sitting out, with not much room for anything other than a table and chairs. Yet such spaces can be utilised to best effect with moveable pots and hanging baskets, as well as the popular window boxes. Herbs can be grown quite successfully this way, even though they never reach their full potential, and an attractive and useful display can be achieved for quite a small outlay.

The kitchen herb garden

When most people think of herbs they think of cooking. The 'pot herbs' were an essential part of flavouring in the days when meats were tasteless and grey: they helped to break down fats and acted as digestives. Nowadays herbs have an infinite number of uses in the kitchen, and so the culinary herb garden where herbs can be gathered fresh is a must for any cook.

A sunny site as near to the kitchen as possible is the ideal location. It doesn't need to be a large garden, but it does need to contain those plants that you most like to use. Having chosen the site, decide upon the shape and size; for example, whether it should be round or square-shaped. Very often herbs are planted among the vegetables as companion plants, and utilise the natural shade and rows in between the vegetables. Tall peren-nials must be allowed plenty of room and placed so they don't mask the lower growing varieties. This may seem obvious, but it is surprising how many, in the desire to plant out quickly, forget this cardinal rule.

In medieval times herbs were planted in strips. This still works well if you are cutting on a regular basis and in large quantities. For the everyday family kitchen a neatly divided bed with chequer board paving or bricks will compartmentalise your herbs and contain them, and at the same time create an attractive display. Pots of herbs can be moved into sunny positions on terraces, and window boxes can contain a small selection for use when the needs are minimal.

If you want to grow herbs indoors it is best to keep them out of the kitchen, or at least away from the cooker, as the grease in the air clogs up the pores in the leaves. An ideal place for indoor herbs is in an airy room or conservatory.

The potager style garden is the most versatile of all kitchen gardens with herbs and vegetables grown in se-lect beds within a very formal setting. The most famous is at Villandry in France. At Villandry there are weep-ing roses at the corners of rectangular beds, like gar-deners tending each plot. The beds are edged with box or wall germander, and plants are displayed in an orna-mental way.

Another type of kitchen garden is the herb spiral. This is a helter-skelter shape using old bricks to create a spiral bed. It creates ideal conditions for different herbs in as small a space as possible. Herbs such as rose-mary that need dry soil can be grown at the top, and moisture-lovers such as chives and garlic are grown at the bottom of the 'slide'. The overall effect is of an ear-ly fortification in miniature, overgrown with herbs.

A number of kitchen herbs are annuals, so allow for spaces among the perennials to grow these. The gaps are not so obvious then in the winter months. Paths from the kitchen to the herbs are essential, and if the beds are quite deep a stepping stone or two helps to get close to plants for cutting.

Opposite: This small front garden with formal brick design is almost obscured by perennial evergreen herbs planted singly in the spaces.
Overleaf: Interesting curves and wedge-shapes add a touch of informality to what is otherwise a very formal herb garden.

The medicinal herb garden

Medicinal herb gardens are also known as physic gardens or apothecary gardens. The traditional physic garden has evolved from the monastic infirmary gardens which were carefully laid out with easily-identifiable herbs grown in separate beds within an enclosed courtyard or fenced surround. Such a herb garden had to

St John's wort is one of the most popular wound herbs – herbs which have healing properties for treating cuts and abrasions. It was associated with the martyrdom of St John, as it yields a blood-red juice when the flowers are steeped in oil and left in the sun to infuse.

provide all the healing plants necessary for the care of the sick both within and without the monastery walls. The hospital was sited at the perimeter of the monastic buildings and apart from it, in order to be able to isolate the contagious and terminally sick. What is little known is that lay women and religious women worked together with the monks in these hospitals, in spite of the closed nature of many of these orders.

At Magdalen College Oxford, a botanical garden was founded in 1621 as part of the school of medicine. Just over 50 years later, in 1674, the Society of Apothecaries in London established the Chelsea Physic Garden, which exists to this day as a centre for study and research into medicinal plants. These gardens, still in existence, have geometrically-ordered layouts, and all plants are labelled so they can be clearly identified.

A number of medicinal plants are shade-lovers, and it is as well to take this into account when planning the position of your herbs. The term *officinalis* denotes medicinal properties, and the fact that the plant has been used traditionally in medicine.

Not all herbs are safe to eat, and some have quite adverse effects on the system, so although the leaf of comfrey is similar to the leaf of foxglove, the actions are quite different. It is, therefore, advisable to keep these two well apart. Decide early on whether or not you are going to grow poisonous plants, and be aware that children are often attracted to the fruit of plants such as deadly nightshade and mandrake.

There is a mystical quality to medicinal gardens in which the plants that are grown have been associated with either magical or spiritual properties, depending on the age in which they were used. Many of the so-called 'magic' herbs have been given Christian names associated with saints and the Virgin Mary, for example lady's mantle, St John's wort and angelica.

It is a good idea to design beds for the medicinal garden that relate to those parts of the body the herbs can treat. Or you can label beds according to the various ailments they treat. And if you planned a 'Culpeper' garden you might arrange beds according to the signs of the zodiac. Whatever you decide, the most important thing to do during the planning and planting stage is to do your research thoroughly and label every plant clearly. Then you can set about a serious botanical study of your private physic garden.

Do not be disheartened by the rather clinical construction of the medicinal herb garden; remember it is the healing properties of these plants rather than their aesthetic properties that matter.

Above: A wall makes a perfect feature for a scented garden, as it reflects heat and retains the scent, in this case the scent of roses. Old-fashioned climbers are particularly fragrant on summer evenings.
Below left: The traditional use of dianthis in scented gardens evokes a sense of history with the dominant scent of these simple yet beautiful flowers. Don't forget to dead-head pinks to encourage more flowers throught the summer months.

The Aromatic Garden

The scented garden is the most romantic of herb gardens. This is a place that invites you to relax and indulge your senses. Old-fashioned roses, banks of thyme, sweet bergamot, pinks – they all conjure up the image of the aromatic garden.

Ideally, the scented herb garden should be quite small, with a seat or grassy bank as its focal point. Always place your seat where the prevailing wind can waft the scents towards you. Surround the garden with sweet-smelling hedges of rosemary, southernwood or lavender. A wattle fence can act as a windbreak on

which you can grow honeysuckle or wild roses. It is essential to enclose the garden to retain the scent. Arbours covered with jasmine or hops will contain the scents around your seat.

Grow ground cover herbs that like to be trodden on, such as pennyroyal, creeping thymes and chamomile. These release their scent when crushed, while others such as winter savory, when planted at the edges of paths, will release their scent when you brush past them. The grey feathery forms of the artemisias invite you to touch them as you pass, and enjoy their unique perfume.

At different times of the year different scents dominate. Early in the summer the subtle scents of the apothecary rose fill the air with soft scent. Later the pinks hit your senses with a rush. Not all scents delight everyone. An aromatic garden is a very subjective garden; what may appeal to one person may be offensive to another, so choose your plants with care and try to experience the pungent aroma of herbs such as santolina when they are in flower, and before you begin to plant them out.

The aromatic garden also depends on colour and form, as it is equally appealing to the eye. Fortunately most herbs have soft pastel colours and the dark green foliage can be mixed with greys and golds. The flowers attract bees, and on a hot summer day it can seem as if all of nature is hard at work while you are relaxing. In the evening the scents are quite different and plants such as evening primrose and woodruff come into their own. By use of grass paths and a chamomile or turf seat you can create a feeling of being in the country even if you are right in the heart of the city. The most important quality to achieve is that of soft femininity. From early times the fragrant herb garden was a place where a lady could escape from the rough world, where lovers could meet in seclusion and where tired minds could find restoration.

If you are planning a garden to supply you with material for pot-pourri then be sure to include a scented geranium such as *graveolens*, *tomentosum*, 'Lady Plymouth' or the lemon-scented *citriodorum*. Although they are quite tender they are vigorous growers and look splendid when grown in isolation in a pot set in

Left: Although old-fashioned roses appear to have a limited life, they are essential in the creation of the romantic scented garden, and continue to please throughout the year if they are carefully collected and dried for use in pot-pourri. If you want roses that flower over a longer period you will have to choose a modern scented variety.

an old chimney pot or on a raised bank. These, together with roses, lavender, lemon verbena, marjoram and bergamot will give you the basis for pot-pourri.

You will need to decide on some arrangement to contain the herbs while at the same time creating the look of an informal setting. Paths are essential, allowing you to pass through the garden and to experience the varied scents. Raised beds sometimes help to enable you to reach plants easily as well as contain them. Utilise all natural features, such as banks or shade-giving trees, and above all keep it simple to begin with. Many annuals will self seed, and weeds should be kept under control, so always arrange your plants so that they can be easily tended and gathered for the home.

Finally, scented gardens are 'secret' gardens and should, if possible, come as a surprise. Entered through a hedge or wall with an attractive gate or soft carpet of chamomile they can always be a place to retreat to or to relax in, where the pace of life slows for a while and your senses are pampered.

The Formal Garden

The traditional concept of the formal herb garden is that of a geometrically-designed formal shape enclosed by box hedging. In many ways it is the easiest to plan, but it can also be the most complicated in design. These complicated patterns have evolved as a result of a fascination with shapes and form that can be achieved by 'knots'. Knot gardens were designed to be looked down upon, either from an upstairs window or from a raised terrace. By interweaving buxus, cotton lavenders and other hedging herbs such as wall germander, it was possible to construct a pattern incorporating motifs or insignia or plain letters.

In a knot garden the shapes are made by close planting and clipping the hedging plants into shape. Over the years buxus has become the favourite for edgings, and because of its lasting evergreen foliage it makes an ideal plant for year-round interest. In Elizabethan times it was fashionable to put different coloured gravels and pebbles between the patterns, and then as new introductions arrived in England they were placed in these spaces in glorious isolation, to show them off. Simple knot gardens can be planted quite effectively, allowing for the fact that when they die down in the winter the garden takes on a clear formal design highlighted by the frosts and snow.

A simple geometric pattern can be just as effective as a knot, incorporating round or square buxus at the

Above: A formal garden created by the author in the south of France, incorporating dwarf box hedging, santolina and rosemary. **Right**: The asymetrical herb garden at Lambeth Palace, London – the residence of the Archbishop of Canterbury – in the process of being replanted. It is interesting to note the bold use of curves and circles.

corners and arranging plants architecturally in the larger shaped beds. A central feature such as an urn or statue helps to focus the design. The balance is all important and cannot be suitably realised without making a very detailed drawing.

The width of paths in relation to shaped beds is vital and the use of brick and stone is greater enhanced by simple patterns such as basket weave and herring bone designs.

Sometimes the most effective formal gardens use very few varieties of herbs. This is particularly noticeable for example in a garden where the only plantings are cotton lavender and lavender trimmed into rounded and square shapes. The contrast in greys is very pleasing to the eye. I have created a simple formal garden in the south of France with dwarf buxus as edging enclosing cotton lavender and cotton lavender *viridis*, clipping the cotton lavender squarely and the *viridis* into mound shapes rising out of the soft grey santolina. The central feature, an Anduse vase, is surrounded by *Rosmarinus officinalis pyramidalis*, and the paths are lawn. Maintenance is minimal, apart from weeding and two or three cuts a year. However as in all formal gardens you must cut off all the flower heads in order to maintain the formal shape.

The formal garden design, in spite of its mathematical restrictions, can be flexible in its approach. With modern design techniques, including the use of computers, new and futuristic patterns might be achieved. Pioneers in garden design in this century included such innovative garden designers as Gertrude Jekyll, who wasn't averse to breaking the mould of so-called 'traditional' patterns; using 'keyhole' effects and inter-locking circles. The possibilities are there for innovative design, and herbs will always decorate and enhance a good formal pattern.

The cottage herb garden

Cottage gardens were intended to be totally self-sufficient, providing vegetables, herbs and flowers for cutting. They were limited in size to the immediate area around the house and as a result were cultivated intensively. This is why they appear to be a bit of a jumble. But in actual fact they were very carefully planted, allowing for the companion planting to deter pests and increase the yield. The vegetable plot would be planted all around with kitchen herbs. Some, such as chives, would deter carrot fly, while others such as chamomile or yarrow would be there to help increase crop yield.

For many years chamomile has been considered to be a 'doctor' plant, helping to strengthen any plants around it. Yarrow makes a good compost activator and soil improver; pennyroyal keeps ants at bay; and nasturtium acts as a trap for blackfly. Mint, borage and basil are all good with tomatoes, and mint is also good

Right: Cottage gardens allow informality to reign supreme. **Below:** In an authentic cottage garden the most important ingredient is a cottage. The older the cottage the better the garden. In this Suffolk garden in England the 16th-century building makes a perfect backdrop.

to plant near cabbages. Tansy, feverfew, wormwood and rue are useful pest repellents, although wormwood should be placed apart from the others and not sited too near roses.

Along the paths in the cottage garden you can plant catmint to provide flower and scent throughout the summer. Winter savory, thyme and hyssop all make good edging borders and pennyroyal, Corsican mint and creeping thymes fill up the cracks in the brickwork. In the herbaceous borders you can mix feverfew, lady's mantle, foxgloves and artemisias with the tall elecampane and fennels among the flowers, allowing chamomile and ladybird poppies to run riot. Borage will self-seed, appearing all over the place each year, and annuals can be sown between rows of vegetables. Roses, pinks, honeysuckle and lilies are perennial favourites in the traditional cottage garden, as are sage, southernwood and all lavenders. Taking into account heights and spread you can fill quite a small area with fragrance and colour that will last throughout the whole of the summer.

The paradise garden

The paradise, or love garden dates back to medieval times. This style of garden was the symbolic representation of the art of courtly love, being the pure love of a knight for his lady and incorporating the devotion to the Virgin Mary and the Christian beliefs that shaped so much of medieval thought as depicted in art and literature. The ideal location would be a castle courtyard enclosed on all sides by the lady's rooms and chapel. This was her private place of recreation far away from the war-like activities of the rest of the castle. The garden was symbolic of her purity, and the only man allowed to penetrate its walls was her husband. The idea originated with the Song of Solomon, in which Solomon recounts the beauties of a perfect sexual union blessed by God.

In a treatise on the soul written in the 4th century, Gregory of Nyssa wrote 'A garden enclosed is my sister, my bride.' This thinking developed into monastic gardens where, symbolically, Christ was the gardener. Water was introduced in the shape of a well or fountain, which represented Christ's wounds, and in the later art the mythical unicorn became the image of Christ's humility and strength. The red rose depicted Christ's blood, shed for mankind, and all these religious images were then woven into the garden style. Every plant in a paradise garden had a symbolic significance.

An exhibition paradise garden at Leeds Castle in southeast England. Note the use of wattle surround to isolate important symbolic plants such as the rue, seen here in the foreground within the basillica-shape created by the low-growing santolina and wall germander hedging.

By Tudor times the secular love garden had taken over with realistic overtones. Here was now a garden to make love in rather than a mystical celebratory love garden. However, it doesn't mean to say that these gardens only existed in literature and art. The paradise garden was real enough for nearly three hundred years, and its simple concept could and does have an impact today. I have created only one Paradise garden, at Leeds Castle in Kent. It was an exhibition garden and existed for its short life in the most perfect setting imaginable. Within the oldest part of the castle is a courtyard adjacent to the queen's bedchamber, with the private chapel and ante chambers at the other sides. There is a marble fountain in the centre. All the right ingredients were there. After turfing over the flagstones we started to experience what it was like to have a little piece of country within the castle walls. A large rue, the 'herb of grace', and spiral buxus to symbolise the unicorn's horn, were placed in wattle surrounds, and two low hedges of santolina and wall germander were set at either end of the rectangular pool in basilica relief. A chamomile seat to one end was flanked by white marguerites and the white flowers of garlic chive. Madonna lilies were put into one corner and the grassy bank under a window planted out with single specimens of rose and white flowers. It wasn't perfect, but it was as near as we could get in early autumn. But the sheer joy was when we turned on the fountain and opened one of the doors from the ante chamber and experienced the simplicity of it all. It felt like turning the clock back, and there was a definite spiritual quality to it all.

A bee and butterfly garden

There is an old tradition that if you rub the inside of your beehive with lemon balm then the bees will never leave. Of all the beekeepers I have met none have vouched for this belief, but all are in agreement that balm, among many other herbs, is beneficial to bees and to the quality of honey.

Bees are attracted by colour, particularly blues, pinks and yellows. So it is essential to have a flowering garden for as long a time as possible. Bees gather nectar from flowers and contrary to belief do not have enormously long tongues, although they do forage from members of the mint family, which have tubular shaped flowers, plants such as thyme, sage, rosemary and, of course, hyssop. Borage is a great favourite with bees as is winter savory and lemon balm. Lavender has produced honey commercially for years, and bergamot, evening primrose, meadowsweet and chives are a must in a well-stocked bee garden.

It is a good idea to choose a very sheltered corner of the garden to place your hive, and plant a rosemary hedge to protect it. Lemon balm and savory are considered good herbs to have close to the hive, and Eleanor Sinclair Rohdes, the American plantswoman and writer, suggests a hedge of sweet briar.

Early in the year wallflowers provide spring nectar and help the hive off to a good start. Butterflies are attracted to paler colours and to them scent is more important than it is to the bees. The Old English types of lavender and pale pinks such as dianthis 'Doris' are more likely to appeal to them.

If you are going to house bees do check their pedigree. I once made the mistake of offering to house a distressed bee colony: it wasn't worth it.

The container herb garden

As far as I'm concerned, plastic is out. Herbs look best in old materials, preferably stone, terracotta or wood. The older the container the better; if you are lucky enough to have antique urns or ancient stone sinks then these are fitting vessels to plant out with herbs. It is an odd fact that these most economical of plants look at their best in expensive antiques. There are, however, excellent stone sinks and terracotta pots on the market that weather well and create the feeling of age quite quickly.

Although it is possible to put four or five herbs into a sink and two or three into a large pot, the best results come from giving the herb a pot of its own. For interest's sake these can be different shapes and sizes, allowing for an ideal depth of 15 cm/6 in, except in the case of creeping thymes and chamomiles. Not so long ago I saw a garden design using drainage pipes set at different

Below: This stone sink illustrates the use of varied forms of colour and height to create a well-shaped planting with architectural plants, such as the dwarf curry plant 'Dartington', as a centrepiece. **Opposite:** French lavender, *Lavandula stoechas*, is most attractive to bees and has the added advantage of flowering early in the year.

By placing herbs in individual pots you allow yourself infinite permutations in shape and pattern. You can also easily move them into sunlight as and when necessary. Be vigilant about watering herbs in pots; terracotta in particular absorbs water, which evaporates quickly.

heights which when planted up looked quite good. But if you want to utilise such things as containers do think about what they will look like in the winter; unless you want a view of interesting drain pipes you may have to consider using evergreen perennials all round. However, old chimney pots look good all the time and provide a suitable height for placing a pot in the top, or an excellent container for keeping mint under control, using plenty of broken pots and stones at the bottom for drainage.

An old sink raised up on bricks can often relieve the overall flatness of a flower border, and there is no reason why you shouldn't mix alpines with small herbs in a sink in a cottage garden setting.

Window boxes, if they are plastic, can be disguised by making a wooden surround and painting this dark green or grey. If you do plant out window boxes do not be tempted to put in tall fennels or lovage, which need deep containers to accommodate their roots, but confine yourself to pot herbs such as thyme, marjoram, chives, parsley, salad burnet and savory. These will produce a good supply for the year. You will have to re-stock the window box annually and feed well during the growing season.

Scented geraniums (pelagoniums) are very rewarding as container herbs and were a great favourite with the Victorians, who filled their porches and front-room windows with enormous specimens. I quite like to add trailing nasturtiums in with the geraniums if the pots are raised up off the ground, so the long-branched stems fall over the edge of the pot and cascade down to the ground.

Hanging baskets can make good containers for herbs but they require a lot of attention and watering. The most successful plantings are the simplest, for example lady's mantle mixed with a dark-blue trailing lobelia. Again, do not be tempted to try anything too large as the soil will not be able to provide enough food or room for the roots.

Large evergreens such as buxus and bay are the most common of the container herbs for permanent planting. Buxus should be placed in straight-sided containers to allow the root formation to develop as naturally as possible. It is important to remember that none of these herbs were ever meant to be cultivated anywhere other than in the ground. It is only the ingenuity and techniques that gardeners have developed that make it possible to establish plants in moveable containers.

Buxus and bay can be pruned into many different shapes and used as architectural features. Spirals,

Right: A bold but economical use of plants often has the strongest effect. These rising spiraling buxus, on an inner-city terrace, need no further embellishment. **Below:** Although this strawberry pot appears to be effectively planted, the lifespan of these herbs is limited. Yearly plantings are essential even when the 'cups' are larger in size.

31

Above: The columnar forms of this bay tree is easily trimmed in early summer and makes a very pleasing architectural shape in large landscapes. **Opposite:** A simple windowbox of culinary herbs – French tarragon, salad burnet, chives, marjoram and thyme – offers a delightful decorative feature to any window sill.

obelisks and pyramid are favourite shapes for buxus, whereas ball shapes on bare trunks of bay make pleasing entrances to porches. Buxus can be clipped into low ball shapes, for variation. It has the added advantage of tolerating shade on north-facing terraces. In the late 17th century it was fashionable to have whole armies of gardeners to change the design of pot-grown plants on terraces into a completely different arrangement while the guests dined, creating a new pattern before the diners returned to the garden for the evening's entertainment.

There are some herbs that benefit from being grown in the house, although I would recommend a light airy conservatory for best results. They are, lemon verbena,

myrtle, sweet basil and pineapple sage. As mentioned earlier, the scented geraniums will grow well inside the house as well as outside. From bitter experience I find that most culinary herbs hate being inside: they need as much ventilation as possible and very careful watering and feeding. Basil, however, likes nothing better than being placed in a hot steamy bathroom with the sun streaming in on it. There are, thankfully, always exceptions to the rule.

With imagination the grouping of containers with colourful and scented herbs can cheer up any terrace or city balcony. If you have a windy balcony it is best to erect some shelter from heavy breezes, over which you can always grow honeysuckle or jasmine to sweeten the air. If you have a roof garden you can spread the weight of pots by using slatted timber, and although I would like to avoid plastic pots there are now some very fine imitations of terracotta in plastic and these would be less likely to put a hole in your ceiling.

Designing a herb garden

Once you have settled on the style of herb garden, the next step is to draw up an initial plan. Because the design of your herb garden is very important, by putting your ideas down on paper using diagrams and drawings, the layout becomes clear and any problems can be overcome before work begins on the site. The plan doesn't have to be an architect's drawing, but in formal designs this is helpful to anybody laying out the hard landscaping. Measurements are vital to create the right balance; and positioning of plants enables you to define shapes and heights.

The plan can take the format of a free-hand sketch, a detail on graph paper, or a full-blown architect's drawing. All of these depend on the size of your garden. If it is a patch of ground near the kitchen to provide just a few culinary herbs, then there is no need to use graph paper – a simple sketch will do. But if the measurements are crucial, which they often are in a formal design, then it is best to resort to this method and draw a plan to scale. Scale rulers are easy to obtain from good stationery suppliers.

Having chosen the position for your herb garden, draw in the boundaries. This will determine whether or not you need extra hedging, fences or walls. Look beyond the immediate area of the site and see what features affect the location. Then measure up the whole area and, after choosing a scale to suit the size of graph paper, outline the shapes and patterns of the herb beds. It is surprising how often the original idea in your head changes once you commit that idea to paper.

Now decide on where the paths and paving should go. This may be old brick, paving slabs or shingle. These items are known as 'hard' landscaping features, which also includes walls, fences, trellis, statuary, water features, containers, seating and steps. Work out where all these items are to go and you are then free to include the plants. These are classed as 'soft' features,

Some herb gardens break away from the symmetrical, geometric shapes of the traditional designs, but they still benefit from an ordered layout with clearly defined walkways and more than one focal point. Such is the case with this garden at Lucas Green, Woking, England, where formality is bordered by an aromatic garden with a seat, and a wild ditch along one boundary. The use of old-fashioned roses grown as standards provides a variation in height, while the open boundary directs the eye around the whole herb garden.

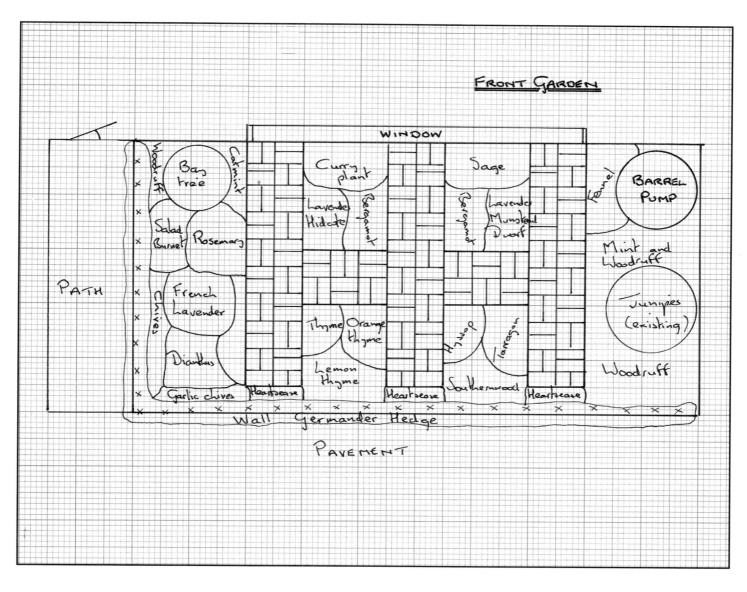

FRONT GARDEN

WINDOW

Woodruff · Catmint · Bay tree · Salad Burnet · Rosemary · French Lavender · Chives · Dianthus · Garlic chives · Heartsease

Curry plant · Lavender Hidcote · Bergamot · Thyme · Orange thyme · Lemon Thyme · Heartsease

Sage · Bergamot · Lavender Munstead Dwarf · Hyssop · Tarragon · Southernwood · Heartsease

Fennel · BARREL PUMP · Mint and Woodruff · Juniper (existing) · Woodruff

PATH

Wall Germander Hedge

PAVEMENT

which is a term covering all plants, trees, shrubs, climbers, hedges and earth features such as banks and mounds. Grass paths and lawns are also termed soft landscaping.

Formal layouts always need low hedges and some focal point such as a statue or urn.

When considering a stylised herb garden the theme may dictate the design. A butterfly garden might be arranged in the shape of a butterfly's wings; for a dye garden you could try to re-create a tapestry using a variety of different coloured flowers; and for a biblical or saints' garden you may wish to incorporate a statue of one of the saints.

The Shakespeare garden is less obvious, but a raised stage could be planted out or beds created using herbs mentioned in separate plays. These are gardens in which to allow the imagination free rein. (For lists of herbs suitable for these gardens see pages 40–41.)

Above: A simple plan drawn on graph paper allows easy planning of a small front garden. By using the squares to plan to scale, the individual bricks can be drawn in. **Below:** A cottage garden may appear haphazard and unruly, but it needs careful planning to achieve a natural effect.

Making a plan for planting is much simpler once you have created the framework. By measuring the spaces in between low hedges and edgings you can then work out how many herbs you can include in each section. The simple chequerboard design with paving slabs (illustrated on page 35) with only one herb to each square makes planning and planting easy, but always be aware of heights, and in such a design either put tall herbs at the centre radiating out in graduated heights, or put tall herbs at the corners. The temptation to cram in as many as possible is overwhelming and I have often added extra plants thinking them small enough for inclusion. But herbs grow quite quickly and reach their optimum heights and widths often in their first season, so be patient and accept the spaces to begin with. They will soon fill in. Use some culinary herbs for borders and allow for shade-lovers and sun-seekers. Mix foliage and flowers to give good variation and always plant some evergreen perennials to offer winter interest.

Right: Not all designs have to be traditional. This abstract pattern is designed to detract from the wedge-shaped area designated for herbs. The use of circles can soften hard edges and the herbs are easily segregated. **Below:** A traditional design with a triangular-shaped bed to one side, for taller kitchen herbs. **Opposite:** The realisation of the plan shown below, one year after it was planted.

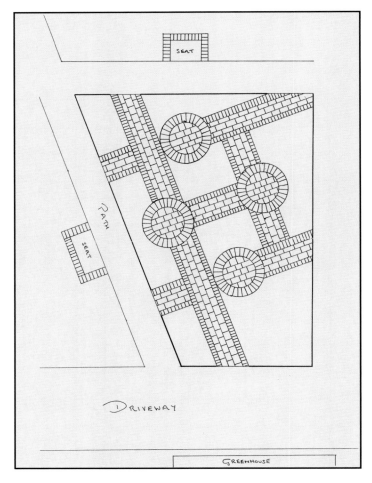

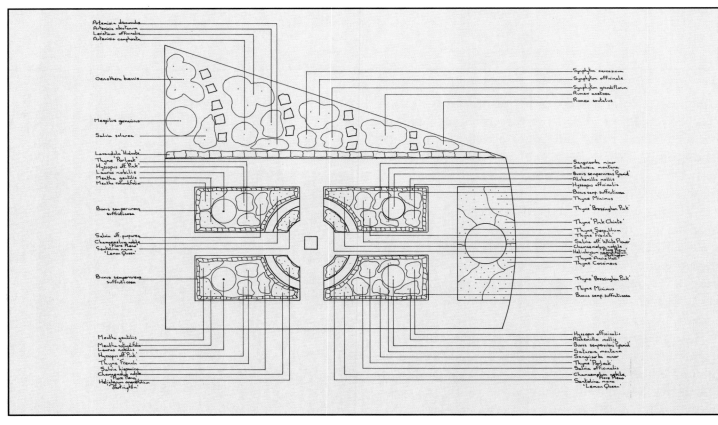

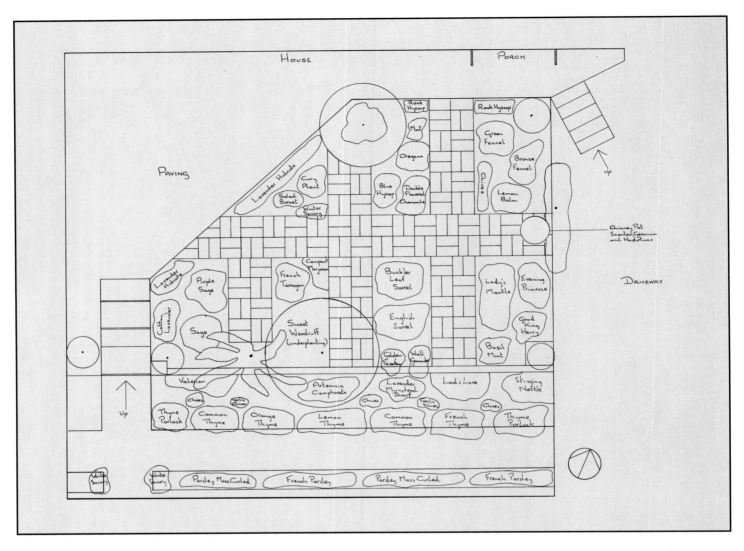

Above: A simple cottage garden plan allows for easy access to all culinary herbs. Note the use of shade-loving herbs beneath the tree.
Opposite above: The beautifully-proportioned knot garden at the Museum of Garden History, Lambeth, London, designed as a tribute to two great plant hunters of the 17th century, the Tradescants, father and son. **Opposite below:** Traditional designs for knot gardens.

Once you have made your plan do not panic. You can always move the plants around the following season to achieve the most pleasing effect if things don't turn out exactly as you had hoped. Design for yourself rather than for others to admire.

Designing a knot garden

If you are planning to make a knot garden then you will need to use all your mathematical and design skills. These herb gardens look very like the patterns on oriental and Persian rugs and were particularly popular in the 16th century, although not everybody liked them. Their critics included Francis Bacon, who was quite scathing when he said: 'As for the making of knots, or figures, with divers coloured earths, that they may lie under the windows of the house on that side on which the garden stands, they be but toys: you may see as good sights many times in tarts.'

Bacon's image of laced pastry on jam tarts is very clear and helps us understand how a garden looks in its interwoven design. This is achieved by using different coloured foliage to give the impression of one hedge passing under another. There are some variegated forms of dwarf box if you wish to keep to one type of plant. Alternatively, wall germander, santolina and rock hyssop make good knot hedges. Having chosen your design then try to keep it on a reasonably small scale; 2 metres/2 yards square should be enough to begin with. However, if you have a flair for draughtmanship then the time taken on an elaborate plan can translate into a fascinating project. An established knot garden is a rare thing, even today, and each and every one is unique and very personal to its creator.

A Biblical/Saints' Garden

Hyssop	Lady's bedstraw
Wormwood	Angelica
Rue	Heartsease
Coriander	Lily of the valley
Pasque flower	Marigolds
Rosemary	Milk thistle
St. John's Wort	Thyme
Costmary	Sweet woodruff
Lady's mantle	

Plus any white-flowered herbs for purity and blue for the colour of Mary's cloak. Some monastic healing herbs such as sage might be included and manger herbs such as pennyroyal and bay for use in herbal wreaths.

A Butterfly/bee Garden

Anise	Lemon balm
Betony	Meadowsweet
Bergamot	Mint
Chives	Rosemary
Comfrey	Sage
Coltsfoot	Thyme
Evening primrose	Valerian
Fennel	Yarrow
Hyssop	Winter savory
Lavender	

A Dye Garden

For yellow dyes
Golden rod
Saffron
Turmeric
Weld
Yellow marigolds

For blue dyes
Dandelion root
Woad

For brown dyes:
Dyers woodruff (root)
Lady's bedstraw
Madder

For green dyes
Bracken
Dock
Lily of the valley
Nettles

For red dyes
Bloodroot
Rose hips
Sorrel

A Shakespeare Garden

From Hamlet,
Ophelia's May herbs
Columbine
Crowsfoot
Daisy
Fennel
Nettles
Pansies
Rosemary
Rue

From
A Midsummer Night's Dream
Cowslip
Garlic
Hawthorn
Hemp
Honeysuckle
Love-in-Idleness
Rose
Sweet eglantine
Thyme

From
The Winter's Tale
Garlic
Lavender
Marigold
Marjoram
Mint
Nettles
Pinks
Rosemary
Rue
Savory

The above list gives just a small selection, but many other Shakespearean herbs can be found by searching through the plays.

Alpine Strawberry

Wife unto the garden and set me a plot
With strawberry rootes of the best to be got;
Such growing abroade, among thornes in the wood
Wel chosen and picked proove excellent good.

Thomas Tussser, *The Proffitable Arte of Gardening* **(1568)**

Botanical name: *Fragaria vesca*
Family: Rosaceae
Other names: Steawberie, sreawbridge, fraise du bois
Life: Hardy perennial

A delicate-leafed spreader that makes a wonderful border plant, sending out runners to invade the territory all around it. Alpine strawberry thrives in woodland and semi-shade, producing tiny, but delicious tasting red fruits. Originally introduced into Europe from Virginia it has been developed by cross-fertilisation into the large fleshy fruit that is today's strawberry. Its name derives from the Old English 'strewbridge', suggesting its ability to strew itself over the ground. John Gerard said of it that 'the distilled water drunke with white wine is good against the passion of the hart, reviving the spirits, and maketh the heart merrie.' It is still considered by medical herbalists to be a good laxative, diuretic and astringent. Linnaeus used its berries as a cure for rheumatic gout. Traditionally, it was used for removing tartar from the teeth, and the juice was also supposed to remove discolouration.

Runners can be divided early in the growing season. The leaves die back in the autumn, but the plant returns doubly revived in the spring. It is a good companion plant to borage, growing well in its natural shade.

Reputedly, wild strawberry is a great culinary favourite in France, where the fruit is picked in the early autumn and served in Parisian restaurants as a delicacy with crême d'Isigny. Related species are: *Fragaria moschata*, also known as musk strawberry. This is a wild plant with larger flowers. Also, *F. virginiana*, the original wild American strawberry, was much used by the North American Indians in herbal medicine.

Angelica

Some call this an Herb of the Holy Ghost, others more moderate call it Angelica, because of its' Angelic Vertues.

Nicholas Culpeper, *The English Physician* **(1653)**

Botanical name: *Angelica archangelica*
Family: Umbelliferae
Other names: Holy ghost root, masterwort
Life: Biennial

A truly architectural plant, angelica can grow to a height of 2 metres/ 6 ½ ft, displaying large umbels of flowers very attractive to bees. I have also found it, sadly, susceptible to blackfly, so keep a close watch for this problem. It can be sown in autumn or divided, and is best planted in rich, well-drained soil allowing for the possibility of light shade. In less sheltered positions its thick stems and stalks may need to be staked. If allowed to flower it dies off quite quickly, so you should regularly clip flower heads if you wish it to take on a perennial nature.

Angelica has a strong tradition as a protective herb against evil and witchcraft. It was, therefore, associated with the archangel Michael, slayer of dragons. This was chiefly because of the fact that it flowers at about the same time of the old festival of St Michael (8 May) and was reputed to have been a powerful remedy against the Great Plague of London in 1665.

Used today more as a flavouring (its stems can be candied) and decoration, it is reputed to be one of the secret ingredients in the liqueur chartreuse. Research has shown it to be rich in medicinal properties giving relief to indigestion, anaemia, coughs, and colds. It is anti-bacterial, anti-fungal, diuretic and an expectorant as well as acting as a stimulant to the circulation. It also induces sweating and has an anti-spasmodic action which helps in treating painful periods. However, in some people it can cause photosensitivity, so although it may appear to be one of nature's 'cure-alls' care should be taken in its medicinal use.

Basil

Most herbs are watered in early morning or at evening, so that they may not be dried up; but basil is watered even at noon, for it is said that it grows more quickly if it is watered with warm water

Theophratus, *Enquiry into Plants* **(300 BC)**

Botanical name: *Ocinmum basilicum*
Family*:* Labiata
Other names: Sweet basil, sweet genovese
Life: Annual

In recent years basil has become an extremely popular herb, probably as a result of advances in greenhouse techniques. It is native to India and requires a hot humid atmosphere in order to thrive. This does not mean to say it cannot be grown outside in temperate climates. Provided it is sheltered from winds and given plenty of light in a rich, well drained soil it will flourish, although not in the luxuriant way of the pampered indoor plant.

I have found it to be a most demanding herb that rewards you well if used regularly and watered morning, noon and early evening in full sun. Do not water at night as it hates to go to bed with its feet wet, and do not be tempted to take too much from it too soon. I have found that the seed germinates quickly when sown in early summer and it will grow on well if transferred to small pots at the four-leaf stage. The seeds are large enough to sow singly in plug trays forming a strong root system before transplanting.

Basil is best torn with the fingers, as tearing imparts a better flavour. Preserved in olive oil with the addition of a little coarse salt, it will provide you with a winter reminder of hot summer days. It is a good idea to keep it apart from rue in the garden. Pinch out the flower heads as soon as they appear and cut hard back in the autumn.

Sweet basil is the most widely used variety and the easiest to cultivate. Others to try are: the dwarf form of bush or Greek basil, and the dark opal purple form. Sacred basil (*Ocinmum sanctum*), known as 'tulsi' in India, is very highly scented.

I have used basil as an insect repellent and have found it to be an excellent tisane when combined with rosemary (1 part basil to 2 parts rosemary) to combat the effects of tiredness.

Bay

Lawrell is appropriate unto triumphs and besides groweth most pleasantly before the gates of the Emperor's court and Bishop's pallace.

Pliny, *Natural Historie* (AD 77)

Botanical name: *Laurus nobilis*
Family: Lauaceae
Other names: Sweet bay, noble laurel, daphne, Roman laurel
Life: Perennial

Anyone who has tasted the leaf fom the bay tree in Provence will tell you of its significant flavour. The warm sun seems to linger within its volatile oils imparting a spicy taste which conjures up images of slopes covered in olive trees, sweet mimosa and vines. The overall feeling of bay is that of goodness, and although it is native to the Mediterranean it will prosper well in northern Europe too. The trees can grow to a height of 12 metres/40 feet; confined to more manageable proportions they can be trimmed into pyramid or ball shapes. At my first nursery I trimmed a 4 metre-/13 foot-high specimen into an umbrella shape and it provided perfect shade for the woodruff growing under it.

A sheltered site is important and you have to be patient in the early years, as laurel grows slowly. A position near the house provides comfort for tree and owner alike. Bay is a herb associated with the Greek god Apollo and with glory. Wreaths have crowned many victorious heads since the days of the Romans. The title 'poet laureate' derives from this use. The herb is said to ward off evil and as such was used for Christmas decoration. It is an evergreen and should not be pruned until early summer. In the event of severe damage by wind or frost, some success has been achieved in cutting the tree right down to the ground in order to help it regenerate.

To dry the leaves, lightly press them under a board and keep out of the sun in order to preserve the essential oils. Store in glass jars rather than bags. **CAUTION**: the variety *Prunus laurocerasus* (cherry laurel) popularly known as 'laurel' is highly poisonous and should not be confused with this beautiful culinary plant.

Bergamot

Speaketh not − whisper not,
Here bloweth thyme and bergamot,
Softly on thee every hour
Secret herbs their spices shower.

Walter de la Mare

Botanical name: *Monarda didyma*
Family: Rustaceae
Other names: Bee balm, Oswego tea, scarlet monarda
Life: Perennial

Bergamot was cultivated extensively by the Oswego Indians of North America. This particular variety is the wild bergamot, *Monarda fistulosa*, which was introduced into Europe in 1656. The leaves and flowers were used to make Oswego tea, a soothing, relaxing tisane with the fragrance of oranges. Confusingly, the flavouring for Earl Grey tea is from the Spanish bergamot orange tree, and although we have taken the name 'bergamot' from that species it is as well to refer to this herb by its botanical name.

The plant we cultivate most often in our gardens today is a related species to the wild bergamot and was introduced in 1752. This is *Monarda didyma* and is most popular with bees, which makes it a must for any garden. The square stems, which grow to a height of 90 cm/39 in, have lanceolate,

serrated leaves with large whorls of red flowers which are particularly attractive to bees. Bergamot prefers to grow in light shade with moist soil; if the soil is not well drained enough the plant tends to be smaller and prone to mildew. The best form of propagation is by root division although seeds can be sown in the spring.

Medicinally, bergamot has been used to relieve flatulence, nausea and painful period pains. There are many varieties of bergamot, offering crimson purple, white or pink flowers. My favourite is 'Croftway Pink.'

The national collection of *Monarda* species is housed at Leeds Castle in Kent, England, under the stewardship of the head gardener Mr Maurice Bristow, who is, in my opinion, one of the kindest experts you are ever likely to meet.

Borage

Borage is called in shops 'Borago': Pliny calleth it Euphrosinum, because it makes a man merry and joyfull: which thing also the old verse concerning Borage doth testifie: 'I Borage bring alwaies courage'.

John Gerard, *The Herball* **(1597)**

Botanical name: *Borago officinalis*
Family: Boraginaceae
Other names: Beebread, starflower burrage, bugloss
Life: Annual

The beautiful, bright blue star-shaped flowers of borage cheer the eye as much as the stems, and fresh young leaves reputably cheer the heart. Once you have borage in your garden you should have it for life as it self-seeds freely. If sown in early spring in a sunny, well-drained soil you should have flowers by July.

If you are very lucky the flowers will appear in early summer, die off and self-seed to produce more flowers during the early autumn. It does not take too kindly to transplanting, so it is advisable to sow in situ or in small pots. Borage is best displayed on a slope where the flowers can hang down, and therefore it makes a good rockery plant.

Borage grows to a height of 60-90cm/ 2-3 feet and has thick hairy stems with rough leaves. Hairs on the underside of the leaves will sting when touched, so be careful when handling it. The herb loses this quality when placed into cordial drinks, flavouring them faintly with just a hint of cucumber. Flowers that have been placed into an ice cube tray make a very attractive addition to summer cocktails and cordials.

Medicinal research has shown that the early herbalists were right to recognise the uplifting qualities of borage. It contains high levels of gamma linoleic acid, useful in many disorders and an aid to blood clotting. It appears to have a stimulating effect on the adrenal glands. This could substantiate the theory that the leaves and seeds help to increase the milk in nursing mothers. As an infusion it has been used for the relief of colds and flu. I enjoy it as a delightful and decorative addition to Pimms No. 1.

Catnip

If you set it, the cats will eat it,
If you sow it, the cats don't know it

Old English Saying

Botanical name: *Nepeta cataria*
Family: Labiatae
Other names: Nep, cat-nep, nepte
Life: Perennial

Having witnessed the delight with which my cats roll about in catnip it is easy to understand John Gerard's description in *The Herball*. He says: 'The later Herbarists doe call it Herba Cattaria, because cats are very much delighted herewith for the smell of it is so pleasant unto them, that they rub themselves upon it, and wallow or tumble in it, and also feed on the branches and leaves very greedily.' It has been suggested by some that it has an aphrodisiac effect on cats. There is a rather charming suggestion in Agnus Castus in the 14th century, saying, 'The vertu of this here is as is if a cat ete thereof it schal conseywyn and brynge forth kytlngis anon.'

If you are not a cat lover this is a herb to avoid in your garden. It is, however, a pretty plant resembling lemon balm with hairy soft leaves, light grey and heart shaped. The white flowers are on soft spikes. It is best propagated by root division in the spring, or you can take cuttings in the summer. These two methods do seem to produce a plant more attractive to my cats. A favourite toy you can make for your cat is a catnip-mouse, using the dried leaf sown into a felt cover.

Medicinally, catnip is a very useful herb for children. Its gentle action in soothing the effects of colds and flu and in relaxing the nervous system make it a useful addition to the first aid cupboard.

Other varieties include *Nepeta mussinii*, the common garden catmint, and the smaller *Nepeta faassenii* both of which make excellent blue-flowering border plants.

Chamomile

There is a remarkable property about the Camomile which some still believe in implicitly – that it is the plant's physician. Nothing is thought to keep a garden so healthy as plenty of Camomile about. It will revive drooping and sickly plants if placed near them.

Frances A Bardswell *The Herb Garden* **(1911)**

Botanical name: *Anthemis nobilis*
Family: Compositae
Other names: Roman chamomile, maythen, ground apple
Life: Perennial

If you wish to plant a chamomile seat, this is the low-growing variety to use. It is a herb that likes to be trodden or sat upon. In recent years, a sterile carpeting variety called 'Treneague' has been developed and this is ideal for using in the making of lawns. Do not, however, be tempted to cover vast tracts with this sweet-smelling herb. The area needs careful weeding beforehand and the ideal size is no more than 6 sq metres/ 64 sq feet.

Although clipping is confined to once or twice in the summer, the chamomile lawn or seat is labour intensive in its upkeep, requiring constant vigilance for weeds and gaps – created by its creeping nature – to be filled. However there is no more fragrant and restful place to sit than on a sunny cultivated lawn or bench of chamomile. This most comforting herb has been loved by gardeners and medical herbalists alike for centuries. It makes a soothing, flavoursome tea and an excellent calming syrup for recalcitrant children. A raised bed of the double flowering, *Anthemis nobilis* 'Flore pleno' was a favourite bed for a visiting vixen to my previous nursery. This somewhat negated the smell of the chamomile, but provided a sanctuary for this useful animal. While she was around I had no trouble from rats or mice. Neither was there any animosity between her and the cats.

There is a wild woodland form of chamomile called Mayweed, or 'stinking chamomile'. This has a foetid smell, which distinguishes it from others. The German chamomile, or matricaria, is an annual and grows much taller than the perennial.

Chervil

Sweet Chervil is so like in taste unto Anis seede that it much delighteth the taste among other herbs in a sallet.

John Parkinson, *Paradisus* **(1629)**

Botanical name: *Anthriscus cerefoluim*
Family: Umbelliferae
Other names: Salad chervil, beaked parsley
Life: Annual

In many ways chervil resembles parsley to look at, but on closer examination you will be able to see that its foliage is more feathery and fernlike. Like chamomile, a lover of well-drained soil, it will grow in most types of soil but prefers a light shade. This can be easily achieved by planting it beneath taller herbs or vegetables. It is a herb that will grow right through the winter months and as such is a very good complementary herb in cooking. It is for this very reason that it is a prime ingredient of the culinary herbs known as *fines herbes*.

If chervil is sown in the cooling days of late summer it can provide two harvests before the end of winter, and early in the following year you can begin successive sowing every month. When harvesting, you should treat it in a similar way to pars-

ley by taking a leaf from the outside. Chervil goes into flower very quickly and then tends to lose its flavour, so cut off the flowerheads before they open. By cutting the plant down to the ground you can assure another crop.

This is not a difficult herb to grow provided you keep it cool and moist. If you are growing from seed, germination will take up to a maximum of six weeks. The seed should be sown in situ. Transplanted seedlings tend to 'bolt' (run to seed) rather quickly.

Chervil is a culinary herb of great importance to chefs and cooks as a prime ingredient for Béarnaise sauce. It also makes a marvellous soup. It can be added to meat, fish, poultry and game as well as omelettes and salads. It is extremely versatile.

Chives

...if they be eaten raw, they send up very hurtful vapours to the Braine, causing troublesom sleep and spoiling of the eyesight.

Nicholas Culpeper, *The English Physician* **(1653)**

Botanical name: *Allium schoenoprasum*
Family: Liliaceae
Other names: Rushe onyons, rush leeks, chibal
Life: Perennial

Chives are known as 'the little brothers of the onion'. They are among the first herbs to show after the winter, pushing their bright green spear-like leaves up from the ground. This is the best time to lift and divide them in order to increase your crop. By dividing the tiny bulbets into clusters of between 8 and 10 you can create a border for the summer. If allowed to flower the stems support globular mauve heads of closely-packed umbels. If you are using chives for culinary purposes it is best to remove the flowers as they create thick woody stems that are inedible, and this also tends to weaken the rest of the plant.

The cylindrical leaves grow to a height of about 25cm/10in and should be cut lightly on a regular basis. This ensures a continual crop throughout the year and helps to avoid yellowing-off at the tips. I find chives grow well in light shade with plenty of moisture. This is one herb that doesn't mind getting its feet wet, and can therefore be grown very effectively near water.

The Romans introduced chives into the British Isles; the herb's other common English name, 'Rush leeks', is the English translation of the Latin name. The mild onion flavour helps to make it a wonderful addition to summer salads. Dried and crushed with a coarse sea salt it makes a chive salt which can be stored in jars. As a member of the garlic family it has a reputation for being a good blood tonic; it is also a useful convalescent herb for children.

The flat-leafed variety known as Chinese or garlic chives has very pretty white flowers similar to wild garlic. Divide large clumps every year otherwise the plant becomes coarse and loses its strong volatile oils, so essential to its flavour.

Comfrey

— if that you put comfrey into a pot wherin flesh is boiling, the peeces of flesh will become no more many but one.

Richard Surflet, *The Countrie Farme* **(1600)**

Botanical name: *Symphytum officinale*
Family: Boraginaceae
Other names: Knitbone, boneset, bruisewort, gumplant, solidago
Life: Perennial

Like all great healing herbs comfrey prefers light shade and will grow very well under trees. Ideally the soil should also be moist, but I have found it will grow quite happily in most soils. It propagates easily by root division, the smallest piece producing a new plant. For this reason it can be quite invasive and may need rooting out every three or four years. The whole plant grows to a height of 100 cm/39 in and is hairy and thick-stemmed. These hairs, as with borage, can be prickly to the touch and I would advise you to wear gloves when harvesting it. By cutting it down on a regular basis through the growing season, comfrey will yield plenty of leaf. It is a good compost herb, helping to break down the layers of waste material and adding rich nutrients to the heap. A liquid feed can be made from this fluid two weeks later. Organic growers find this a most useful plant for mulching, feeding and composting. Comfrey was introduced into England from Russia in 1871 by Henry Doubleday, who was the great pioneer of organic gardening.

The roots and leaves of comfrey can be used in herbal medicine. The presence of up to 0.8 per cent allantoin helps it to promote healing of fractured bones and bruises. It can be used as a poultice for varicose ulcers and as a compress for varicose veins. It has also helped in the treatment of bronchial complaints.

There are two smaller forms of comfrey that I like to grow in the garden: *Symphytum grandiflorum*, a dwarf variety with pink and cream flowers, and *S. caucasicum* with striking blue flowers.

Some caution should be exercised in the use of comfrey as a tisane, as research has shown it to have a carcinogenic effect on the liver.

Coriander

*Coriandre layd to wyth breade or barly
mele is good for Saynt Antonyes fyre.*

William Turner, *A Newe Herball* **(1551)**

Botanical name: *Coriandrum sativum*
Family: Umbelliferae
Other names: Cilantro
Life: Annual

Coriander is a herb with world-wide popularity. Pliny claimed the best to be from Egypt, where it was used extensively as a medicinal plant. Seeds of coriander were found in Tutankhamun's tomb. Maude Grieve, in her *Modern Herbal* (1931) tells us that in Peru it is so much liked that it 'enters into almost all their dishes'. Anyone who has been to an Asian market knows of the enormous bunches to be had there.

If your climate is dry and hot then this is an easy herb to grow. If you are likely to suffer a wet, cold period in summer then don't be disappointed if you have crop failure. Sow once there is no fear of frosts and thin out seedlings to about 15cm/6 in, allowing for the fact that the feathery leaves need support. Dill is a good companion plant and can offer the support needed. Either that or grow in full rows or clumps. The soil should be well-drained and sunny. Successive sowing is best as it goes to seed quite quickly. Forms such as coriander 'Cilantro' that put all their energies into producing leaf are available, but even these are prone to bolt eventually. The ball-like seeds, however, are important for culinary use, and maintain their flavour for a long time. Coriander has been used for many years as a digestive herb and for the relief of flatulence.

Pliny also recommended its use as an antidote for the 'poison of the two-headed sperpent', also with honey and raisins to heal spreading sores, for diseased testes, burns, carbuncles, sore ears and fluxes of the eyes. He suggests making a drink of coriander and rue for cholera and using the seed for expelling intestinal parasites, all of which demonstrates the fact that this is not a good subject for conversation before breakfast.

Costmary

It is an especial friend to evil, weak and cold livers.

Nicholas Culpeper *The English Physician* **(1653)**

Botanical name: *Balsamita major tanacetiodes*
Family: Compositae
Other names: Alecost, balsamita, balsam herb, maudlin
Life: Perennial

Costmary, or alecost, can grow up to a 45cm/18in high. The leaves are finely toothed, entire in shape and have a delightful balsam scent. This herb was used in medieval times for flavouring beer, from which it derives its name. I was first encouraged to grow costmary having learned of its use as a bookmark for bibles. It acts as a sweet antidote to musty-smelling books, the scent lasting for many months, with the herb taking on a paper-thin translucent quality when dried between the pages. The tiny clusters of yellow flowers in late summer are insignificant.

Costmary will grow in almost any soil and can be divided in the spring or autumn; it should be placed at least 60cm/24 in apart to allow it sufficient room to spread. I have found it unable to cope with hindrance from other plants which grow in close proximity.

In France it is known as herbe Sainte-Marie and is dedicated to Mary Magdalene, giving rise to the country name of 'Maudlin'. It is said to help clear catarrh when taken as a tisane and has been used as both a strewing herb and as a tasteful and aromatic addition to salads.

Camphor is a similar plant which looks strikingly like costmary. Its botanical name is *Balsamita vulgaris* 'Tomentosum', and it grows to a height of 1 metre/39 in. It has white daisy-like flowers and the foliage smells strongly of camphor. There is also a golden variety of costmary called *T. parthenium* aureum, which has white flowers and grows to a height of 45cm/18 in.

Cotton Lavender

It is planted in Gardens to border knots with, for which it will abide to be cut into what forme you think best, for it groweth thick and bushy.

John Parkinson *Paradisus* **(1629)**

Botanical name: *Santolina chamaecyparissus*
Family: Compositae
Other names: Lavender cotten, santolina
Life: Perennial

The branched silver-grey, coral-like stems of santolina make it a most decorative feature for any border edge. I like to mix it with the dark green variety, 'Rosmarinifolia viridis' and clip the plants into flat and ball shapes. Providing you cut santolina hard back in the spring to the new growth showing at the base of each stem, then, as John Parkinson suggests, you will be rewarded with bushy plants, ideal for low hedging. The tiny yellow button flowers are particularly striking, forming a heavily scented carpet of flower above the woody stems. The smell is not to everyone's liking, being pungent and rather heady. If the flower heads are removed the bushy growth is stronger and can be shaped.

To propagate, take cuttings in spring or autumn and set them in sharp sand. Like rosemary, the plant can be layered. It is a 'dry' herb that prefers a light soil which drains well, and it needs full sun. Traditionally it has been used as a vermifuge (used to expel intestinal worms) and moth repellent, and as a tisane, but it has no culinary use.

Other varieties include *S. chamaecyparissus* 'Nana' a more compact form growing only 30cm/12 in in height with coarse silver foliage and yellow flowers; Santolina 'Lemon Queen', which has softer creamy yellow flowers and a heavy scent, 'Lambrook Silver' and another *S. viridis* form called 'Primrose Gem'. Sometimes *S. viridis* is listed as *S. rosmarinifolia*.

Dill

Brings relef to a stomach that is cold and windy.

Tacinum Sanitatis, **The Medieval Health Handbook** (*c.* **1345**)

Botanical name: *Anethun graveolens*
Family: Umbelliferae
Other names: Dillseed, dillweed, anetum
Life: Annual

I have long since given up growing dill in small pots for selling on. It is not fair to the plant and it is not fair to the customer. Dill does not take kindly to transplanting and goes to flower very quickly as a protest. Since you tend to grow dill for its delicate, feathery leaf then a wiser strategy is to purchase a good seed, such as Dukat, and grow in situ.

Dill needs a light soil in a sunny position protected from winds. It grows to a height of 50-90cm/24-36 in. The leaves are blue-grey in colour and the dark green stalks bear four umbels of yellow florets. Sow in the spring and then sow successively for two more months. Avoid growing near fennel as the two plants cross-pollinate easily. Dill is also known to have an adverse effect on carrots and tomatoes.

The name originates from the old Norse word 'dilla', meaning 'to lull'. This may account for its use for many years as an ingredient of gripe water, used as a remedy for colic in babies.

Dill is used especially in the pickling of cucumbers, and is also mainly associated with a sauce for fish and as a flavouring for bland vegetables. Its reputation for stimulating the appetite, as well as assuaging hunger, gave it the name 'meeting house', as during the 17th and 18th centuries the seeds were chewed to alleviate the boredom of long dry sermons.

The only related species is *Anethum sowa*, known as Indian, or Japanese, dill, which is used as an ingredient in Asian cooking.

Evening Primrose

Evening primrose seeds itself to distraction, but the large pale-yellow flowers which open at night also add delicious perfume to the evening hours, and are not despised.

Margery Fish, *Cottage Garden Flowers* **(1961)**

Botanical name: *Oenothera biennis*
Family: Onagraceae
Other names: Tree primrose, evening star, king's cure-all
Life: Biennial

In recent years it came as some surprise to the scientific world that this garden 'escape' plant should have kept its secrets for so long. The essential oils of this strikingly beautiful herb were found to contain large quantities of gammalinoleic acid. Research, which is still continuing, has shown that this substance is effective in the treatment of blood clotting, pre-menstrual tension (PMS), arthritis, eczema, liver damage caused by alcohol abuse and countless other benefits to our well-being.

In the garden evening primrose makes a beautiful backdrop to a border, particularly if there is a wall or wattle fence behind it. The plant grows to a height of anything up to 1.5metres/5 ft with yellow trumpet-shaped flowers starting from the top of the plant in mid to late summer. The flowers look well in the evenings, giving rise to the common name; the individual flowers survive only for a day but others are produced further down the stems. Seed capsules develop when the flowers fade, guaranteeing plants for the next season.

Evening primrose will grow in most soils, providing there is good drainage, and prefers sun although it is quite happy in light shade too. Seeds should be sown in early summer so that the young plantlets can be set out in autumn for flowering the following year.

The roots of evening primrose have been used as a vegetable and the flowers make a pretty ingredient for salads, a common usage in France.

Fennel

Fennel deserves high praise both for its taste and smell. It is good for weak eyes.

Walafrid Strabo, *The Little Garden* **(1840)**

Botanical name: *Foeniculum vulgare*
Family: Umbelliferae
Other names: Finkle, fenkle, sweet fennel, wild fennel
Life: Perennial

Fennel, with its tall fronds of green feathery leaves, looks splendid at the back of a border. I particularly like the bronze form standing in front of a golden hop. The flowers grow in yellow umbels, allowing the plant to grow up to a height of 2 metres/6 ft. For a continual supply of leaf through the summer it is best to keep cutting the plant down to prevent it going to seed. It is not a very good companion herb for coriander and should not be grown near dill as it is likely to cross-fertilise. The old saying 'Fennel for your kennel' originated from its reputation as a flea repellent, but could well have suggested that this is also an ideal way to keep it away from other plants.

The Greeks called fennel 'marathon' meaning to grow thin. Whether this had anything to do with running 26 miles or was so called because of its dis-

tinctive qualities I am not sure. According to Greek legend, Prometheus stole a spark from the fire on Mount Olympus and hid it in the stalk of a fennel. Revered by the Romans as a strength-giving herb, fennel was also considered good for the eyes, and is still used today as an eyewash for sore and tired eyes.

Sow seed or divide the roots of an established plant in the spring. Do not confuse with Florence fennel, which is a vegetable grown for its bulbous root. Common fennel is useful as a good anise flavouring for fish dishes and for soups and stews. The leaves can also be used raw in salads.

Related species are *Foeniculum vulgare purpureum*, known as bronze fennel, and *F. vulgare*, Florence fennel, which is an annual cultivated for its succulent root.

Feverfew

In the worst headaches this herb exceeds
whatever else is known.

Sir John Hill, *The British Herbal* **(1772)**

Botanical name: *Tanacetum parthenium*
Family: Compositae
Other names: Featherfoil, flirtwort, bridesmaids' buttons
Life: Perennial

If ever there was a herb that fitted the description of a plant that 'grows like a weed', it's feverfew. For the many migraine sufferers who have found relief from eating the leaves it is just as well. This pungent, daisy-flowered garden escape demands a certain amount of respect. For although it can help to reduce the effect of migraine the leaf should be taken in very small quantities and rolled in a pellet of bread to avoid mouth ulcers. If you are unfortunate enough to suffer in this way then try using tincture of myrrh as a remedy. A tea made from feverfew leaves and flowers can sometimes help with depression.

There are other varieties of feverfew to grow in your borders. The golden form adds a splash of brightness, and the double-flowered variety also helps to offer new interest. All feverfew are very easy to grow, although I have found them suscep-

tible to blackfly. A regular spray with Derris can usually eradicate this problem, and keep the plant safe to eat. It self-seeds freely, can be increased by root division in the spring and will grow quite well from cuttings taken in the autumn and early spring.

Feverfew has been used as an insect repellent. Traditionally, it was grown near buildings, in the belief that it would ward off evil spirits and disease. It is one of the first herbs to flower in the year and I use it as a plant to fill in gaps that have been left after the winter.

Related species are: *Tanacetum parthenium aureum*, known as golden feverfew, with striking yellow foliage and daisy white flowers. Also, a rarer double-flowering form, *T. parthenium* 'Double', which has white pom-pom flowers all summer. The leaf of both of these varieties can be used by migraine sufferers.

Foxglove

It has been found by experience to be available for the King's evil ... I am confident that an ointment of it is one of the best remedies for a scabby heart that is...

Nicholas Culpeper, *The English Physician* **(1653)**

Botanical name: *Digitalis purperea*
Family: Crophulariaceae
Other names: Bloody fingers, dead men's bells. Virgin's glove, fairy thimbles, fairy caps
Life: Biennial

The large number of different varieties of modern foxglove make this a must for any herb garden, in spite of the fact that every part of it is poisonous. It is amazing to think that not many deaths were recorded from the use of digitalis before the discovery by Doctor William Withering, in the late 18th century, of its stimulating effect on the heart. Today, the heart drug digitoxin is produced from *Digitalis purpurea*. This is such a powerful herb that it should only be used under the guidance of a qualified medical herbalist or doctor.

Foxglove is tremendously attractive to bees. The flowers do not appear until the second year, when they rise on long spikes from a rosette of thick, downy leaves. John Gerard describes them as 'set in a course one by another upon one side of the stalke, hanging downwards with the bottome upward, in forme long, like almost to finger stalkes,

whereof it tooke his name "*Digitalis*".'

It is worth noting that although bees and other insects visit the foxglove and use it for shelter on wet, cold days, other animals, by instinct, do not graze on foxgloves. Our fox never went near them, so proving the corruption of the word from 'Folksglove'. The only legend that points to the fox comes from Norway, where the bad fairies were supposed to cover the fox's paws with the flowers in order to soften the sound of his tread.

Two varieties worth considering are the woody foxglove *D. lanata*, which has white flowers, and the yellow-flowered foxglove *D. lutea*. They are both only 50cm/18ins in height. *D. purpurea* can grow to a height of 2 metres/6 feet. Ideal conditions are a hot, sunny, well-drained bank protected by trees. Its natural habitat is woodland, so plenty of leaf mould helps it to thrive well.

Good King Henry

Good King Henry was the name given to distinguish the plant from another, a poisonous one, called Malus Henricus ('Bad Henry').

Rembert Dodoens, *A Niewe Herball* **(1578)**

Botanical name: *Chenopodium Bonus Henricus*
Family: Chenopodiaceae
Other names: English mercury, fat hen, poor man's asparagus, goosefoot, smearwort
Life: Perennial

An early-growing spinach substitute, good king henry thrives on a deeply dug, well cultivated soil in partial shade or full sun. French legend would have us believe that the name was derived from a decree by Henry IV of France that all peasants should have a weekly fowl to eat. This chicken was fattened and stewed with the herb, and this would help to explain its country name 'fat hen'. Because of this kindly action, Henry IV is still thought of with affection by the working people of France.

After the first year, cut the leaves on a regular basis to encourage the plant to regenerate. It is best grown from seed in spring, in situ, and doesn't like being transplanted. In summer it produces tiny clusters of pale yellow flowers on coarse stems. These should be cut off to ensure a plentiful supply of leaf. Traditionally, good king henry has been used for poultices to treat sores, and the leaves were used to aid digestion. The leaves resemble a goose's foot, a fact reflected in both the English name 'goosefoot', and in the Latin name *chenopodium*, derived from the Greek for 'goose foot'.

Two closely related species are common orache, or iron root, *Atriplex patula*, and American wormseed, *C. ambrosiodes*. Common orache is native to Britain, where it grows on wasteground: American wormseed is native to tropical regions of America, from where it was introduced into Europe. Like good king henry, this plant has medicinal uses. It has antispasmodic qualities and has been found to be useful in the treatment of asthma, nervous ailments and menstrual disorders. It is also known to expel worms living in the intestine. However, this herb should only be used under medical supervision as both the plant and its oil can be toxic in large doses.

Hyssop

*Cleante Hyssop is an hearbe to purge and clense
Raw flegmes, and hurtful humours from the brest,
The same unto the lungs great comfort lends,
With hony boyl'd: but farre above the rest
It give good colour, and complexion mends,
And is therefore with women in request.*

Sir John Harrington, *The Englishman's Doctor* **(1607)**

Botanical name: *Hyssopus officinalis*
Family: Labiatae
Other names: sope, hissop, hysope
Life: Perennial

It is well worth the wait for hyssop flowers to appear in mid to late summer. The deep blue whorls on tall, fragrant spikes are much loved by bees. Grown in large groups hyssop has a heady effect on the senses. It makes a good hedging plant but often at the expense of the flowers. I prefer to grow the smaller 'rock hyssop' for this purpose. You can allow it to grow to its full height of about 30cm/12in, having planted it no more than 20cm/8in apart. The flowers are even deeper in colour than the ordinary hyssop.

It has been suggested that this dwarf form, *Hyssopus aristatus*, could be the hyssop referred to in the bible. Psalm 51 verse 7, reads: 'Purge me with Hyssop, and I shall be clean.'

One drawback to cultivating hyssop, which likes a dry, well-drained soil with full sun, is that it tends to go woody and needs replacing every four years. But it produces plenty of seed, which is easy to harvest, and cuttings can be taken before flowering in the summer.

There is a bitter constituent in hyssop called 'marrubin', which gives it its expectorant qualities. Taken as a tisane it can be beneficial in treating upper respiratory infections and chest complaints. Sprinkled on meats it helps to break down the fat. It is not as popular today as a culinary herb, but it remains an important ingredient in a famous liqueur, chartreuse.

Of the pink and white forms of hyssop I find that the white form grows better for me. But that may depend on conditions such as the local climate and the situation.

Lady's Mantle

Lady's Mantle is very proper for those wounds that have inflammation...

Nicholas Culpeper, *The English Physician* (**1653**)

Botanical name: *Alchemilla vulgaris*
Family: Rosaceae
Other names: Lion's foot, bear's foot, nine hooks, Stellaria
Life: Perennial

Lady's mantle is one of nature's 'magic' herbs, dedicated to Mary, mother of Jesus, by the early Christians. Its name, however, derives from the Arabic word 'alkemelych' meaning alchemy. It was recognised from very early times as a wondrous healer, and it is easy to appreciate the reverence with which it was kept when you see, early in the morning sun, the tiny spherical droplets of dew on its cloak-shaped leaves. This is as good a reason as any to include it in your herb garden, but I have grown borders of this graceful plant more for its frothy yellow flowers, which stand only 30 cm/12 in above the soft green leaves. It increases each season so be careful to divide the roots either in spring or late autumn so that it does not become overcrowded. It will also self-seed freely. In the wild it is often found in shady woodlands, but it will grow well in full sun too.

Medicinally, lady's mantle is classed as a 'woman's' herb. It has been used most effectively to strengthen the womb and is therefore considered by medical herbalists to be a good tonic to aid in conception. It has also been used in the treatment of painful periods, and before and after childbirth. The gentle visual look of this beautiful herb seems to suggest its caring qualities. Traditionally it was used as a 'wound' herb.

Lady's mantle is a favourite with flower arrangers as it makes a soft contrast to strong leaf forms. The dwarf form, *Alchemilla alpina,* makes a very pretty addition to a small sink or trough.

Although I look upon this herb as a safe herb, I would never advise self-medication in cases of pregnancy. Always consult a registered medical herbalist or doctor who will prescribe a carefully formulated tincture and monitor your progress.

Lavender

I judge that the flowers of Lavender quilted in a cap and dayly worne are good for all diseases of the head that come of a cold cause and that they comfort the briane very well.

William Turner, *A Newe Herball* **(1551)**

Botanical name: *Lavandula angustifolia,* syn. *officinalis*
Family: Labiatae
Other names: English lavender, true lavender
Life: Perennial

There are many varieties of lavender, but the one with the strongest scent and the most volatile oils is the English lavender, cultivated extensively in Norfolk, England, and famously in the Provence region of France. There it is known as 'French lavender' a name given in this country to *Lavandula stoechas*, a smaller form with ornamental purple bracts rather than the whorls on longer stems characteristic of *angustifolia*.

Lavender flowers throughout the summer and should be harvested on a dry day soon after the sun has dried the early morning dew off the leaves. It is much loved of bees and for this and other reasons no garden should be without a bush of lavender. It can be clipped into a hedge, but care should be taken not to cut back into old wood.

There are two schools of thought about when to prune lavender, spring or autumn. I prefer to cut off all the spikes in early autumn and then wait until the new spring growth is showing before shaping the bush. This will also give the bush a chance to build up its strength for the new year. Early autumn, however, is a good time to take hardwood cuttings. Growing from seed takes a long time.

Lavender derives its name from *lavare*, which is Latin for 'wash'. Thought of even today as a herb for the bath it has great cleansing properties. Lavender water makes a refreshing face wash, and a bowl of lavender flowers sweetens a room when disturbed by the fingers. Spikes of lavender used to be burned in the fireplace to fumigate a sick room.

Of the many varieties, I particularly like 'Hidcote', a smaller bush with deep blue flowers, and 'Munstead Dwarf', ideal as a low border. The lavender *soechas* , or French lavender, is well worth growing for its scent and unusual flowers.

Lemon Balm

Balm, hot and dry, cordial and exhilarating, sovereign for the brain, strengthening the memory, and powerfully chasing away melancholy.

John Evelyn, Acetaria (1699)

Botanical name: *Melissa officinalis*
Family: Labiatae
Other names: Bee balm, melissa, sweet balm
Life: Perennial

John Hussey of Sydenham breakfasted every morning for 50 years on lemon balm tea sweetened with honey. He died at the ripe old age of 116. Is it hardly surprising that lemon balm is classed as a 'long life' herb? Melissa, as it is often called (meaning 'bee' in Greek) is a delightful lemon-scented member of the mint family and is one of the easiest herbs to grow. It self-seeds freely and will root from the smallest piece. As a result it can be quite invasive and needs to be kept in check.

The best way is to cut it hard back before it gets a chance to flower in mid-summer. You can clip it into ball shapes at about this time too. The leaves are oval-shaped and finely toothed with a strong scent of lemon. Because of this they make wonderful additions to salads and summer drinks.In the 17th century, in the time of William Shakespeare, lemon balm was much in favour as a herb for polishing furniture.

The Carmelite nuns created an elixir tonic called Carmelite Water using brandy, nutmegs and angelica root with lemon rind and the leaves of lemon balm. You can use the leaves for summer drinks, salads and desserts. The fresh leaves make a refreshing tisane. To make a sleep-inducing tea infuse equal parts of chamomile flowers, lemon balm and St John's wort.

Balm oil and hot water infusions have been used externally to treat shingles. As it induces sweating it makes a very useful treatment for colds and flu. It also reduces blood pressure.

Beekeepers have grown lemon balm near hives for generations because of its abundant nectar, and there is an old theory that a hive rubbed inside with the leaves will never lose its bees.

Lemon Verbena

In English, Juno's teares, Mercuries moist bloud, Holy-Herbe.

John Gerard, *The Herball* **(1636)**

Botanical name: *Lippa citriodora*
Family: Verbenaceae
Other names: Kerb Luisa, Spanish thyme, *Aloysia triphylla*, lemon-scented verbena.
Life: Perennial

Lemon verbena is native to Chile. As a result it needs a very warm sheltered climate in order to survive cold winter months. It is best grown in a large container and brought in at the first sign of frost. It is the most fragrant of all the lemon scents in the garden and therefore makes a tasty addition to summer desserts and drinks. The sedative effect of a tea infused from the leaves has made it a most popular calming tisane to take at night or after meals.

Lemon verbena forms quite a tall shrub that can be trained against a wall or grown as a corner feature in a conservatory. The leaves are pointed, long and narrow. It will grow well in a light, well-cultivated soil and requires very little attention except in the late autumn, when a mulch can be beneficial in protecting its roots for the winter. Harvest and dry the leaves at the time of flowering and store in airtight jars. The leaves will retain their flavour well. It has been used in finger bowls and the oil extracted from the herb is used for making soaps and perfume.

Lemon verbena is often confused with *Verbena officinalis*, which is called 'vervain' in some countries. The confusion arises from the fact that lemon verbena is called 'verveine' in France, used to relieve nausea, flatulence and dyspepsia.

The olfactory memory in many children brought up by Victorian nannies was that of lemon verbena, which they associated with their mothers, who would place a leaf of the herb between the breasts to act as a natural deodorant when wearing a ballgown. When the rarely-seen mother went to the nursery to kiss the chilren before leaveing for the evening, the all-prevading scent filled the air long after her departure.

Lovage

If Saturn offend the throat (as he always doth if he be the occasion of the malady, and in Taurus is the genesis) this is your cure.

Nicholas Culpeper, *The English Physician* **(1653)**

Botanical name: *Levisticum officinale*
Family: Umbelliferae
Other names: Love parsley, old English lovage, bishop's weed, king's cumin
Life: Perennial

Mrs C F Leyel, celebrated champion of herbal medicine in the 1940s, lists lovage as a 'herb to control pain'. This referred to its traditional use in relieving rheumatic pain. Thought of today more as a culinary herb, lovage has a long history, beginning with its introduction into Europe from India. It was reputed to have aphrodisiac properties and was worn as a love charm in Eastern Europe. A monastic herb in the Middle Ages, it has been suggested that lovage was used to give protection against the plague.

I grow lovage at the back of borders as it can grow as high as 2 metres/6 feet. It is quite striking when it comes into flower during mid-summer, with umbrella-shaped yellow flowers on long stems. The leaves are bright green and broad in shape. Because of its size and large rootstock it is advisable to plant it in a rich, deep, well-drained soil, giving the roots a chance to seek water. One plant will supply a family's needs for the year, by cutting back several times during the summer months. It is easily increased by root division in the autumn or very early spring. Seeds can be sown under glass in the spring. The soil around young plants should be kept moist.

The leaves are used to flavour soups, or to make into a soup on their own. They are also used to flavour casseroles and any sauce that needs a light celery flavour. The stems can be candied, like angelica. The large leaves also make useful additions to flower arrangements.

Although medical herbalists use lovage as a warming digestive tonic and to treat menstrual problems, it has been shown to have an adverse effect on diseased kidneys. It should also be avoided during pregnancy.

Marigold

Others name it the Sunne's Bride, and Sunne's hearbe ... for the decking of Garlands bewitfying of Nosegayes, and to be worn in the bosom.

Thomas Hyall, *A Most Briefe and Pleasaunt Treatyse* **(1563)**

Botanical name: *Calendula officinalis*
Family: Compositae
Other names: Pot marigold, calendula, golds, ruddes
Life: Annual

Pot marigold is a favourite of cottage gardens, primarily because of its colour, but also because it grows easily and rewards the gardener with flowers throughout the summer months and well into the autumn.

Sown in a light soil and thinned out to at least 45 cm/18 in apart marigolds make a lovely border. As the flowers die off you should dead-head them so that more will appear. The orange or yellow flowers grow on single stems; the petals can be used to decorate salads most effectively.

Pot marigold has always been associated with the sun, and Charles I of England is reputed to have said: 'The marigold observes the Sun/ More than my subjects me have done.'

Pot marigold is a great natural healing plant, a warm, friendly herb with soft hairy leaves and resinous feel. It has anti-inflammatory, antiseptic, anti-fungal actions, which makes it an excellent 'wound' herb, good for oral thrush, throat infections, leg ulcers, excema, mouth ulcers, inflammation of the middle ear and for clearing the fallopian tubes. It also relaxes spasms and generally cheers the heart.

Historically, marigold also has a dark side: it is associated with jealousy, probably because of its resemblance to the emblematic shields worn on the left arm of fighters in Provence. There the marigold is called *gauchefer*, and Chaucer refers to the flowers being worn as a jealous garland. Marigolds derive the name *calendula* from the Greek word 'kalends', referring to the first days of the month when plant was reputed to be in flower. Its virtues are considerable and it self- seeds freely, assuring a good crop the following year. In fact the self-sown marigolds flower early.

Marjoram

*Marierum is a thicke and bushy herbe…it hath a
very good savour.*

William Turner, *A New Herball* **(1551)**

Botanical name: *Origanum majorana*; also *O. onites* and *O. vulgare*
Family: Labiatae
Other names: Sweet marjoram, amaracus, joy of the mountain
Life: Perennial

I have included oregano under this heading as it is of the same family. The name oregano comes from two Greek words meaning 'joy of the mountains', and is a herb associated with happiness. It was planted on graves as a cheerful farewell and given to couples in a wedding garland.

There are several varieties of marjoram, the most often seen being sweet marjoram, also known as knotted marjoram, pot marjoram, golden marjoram, gold-tipped marjoram and the wild marjoram, known as oregano. All are perennial, although strictly speaking sweet marjoram is a tender perennial best grown annually each spring. They all prefer dry, fertile soil with plenty of sun.

Marjoram is a bushy, shrub-like plant with oval leaves on woody stems. The mounded cushions of pot marjoram, most striking in the golden marjo-ram, make useful shapes on higher and sloping ground, although they tend to fall away from the centre when in flower. The flowers of oregano grow in mauve clusters and have a heady, musty scent and are most attractive to bees. As a result oregano was a popular strewing herb and was used in nosegays, as well as being used to scour furniture. Marjoram has also been used in hair tonics and in snuff, and is reported to have a beneficial effect on the brain. Its culinary uses are for stuffings in sausages, meat and poultry, and flavouring for soups. I also like to add a few leaves to salads.

Traditionally, marjoram was used for flavouring beer, and it also has good digestive qualities. I like to use it in digestive tonics, steeped in wine. It is the bitter constituents of this herb which aid digestion and prepare the stomach before eating.

Meadowsweet

Queen Elizabeth of famous memory did more desire it than any other sweet herbe to strew her chambers withal.

John Parkinson, *The Theatre of Plants* **(1640)**

Botanical name: *Filipendula ulmaria*
Family: Rosaceae
Other names: Queen of the meadows, meadwort, meadsweet, dollof, bridewort
Life: Perennial

Meadowsweet is often referred to as 'nature's aspirin'. This is because it contains salicylic acid in its flowerbuds and it is this constituent that was isolated from the plant and made into the drug we know today as 'aspirin'. This name comes from the herb's old botanical name *Spirea ulmaria*. What is interesting to note is that while aspirin causes the stomach lining to bleed, if meadowsweet is used the other constituents of the plant help to relieve stomach acidity. This is probably one of the best examples of holistic medicine that traditional methods can show.

Meadowsweet flowers have a delightful vanilla scent and make a most pleasant drink at night. It has been shown to have an anti-depressant effect.

In the wild it grows in shady areas by streams and on moist banks, and when in flower has a fluffy cloud-like appearance. It stands up to 1.25

metres/4 feet in height with reddish stems and decorative pinnate leaves. The frothy flowers appear in mid to late summer. In the garden you can plant it where it will get plenty of moisture, in full sun or partial shade. Seed is best sown in situ and it can be propagated by root division in the spring. The herb was often used as a strewing herb, and was made into mead sweetened with honey. It was also used as a flavouring in beer.

Meadowsweet was one of the most sacred herbs of the Druids, and Elizabeth I gave it her royal blessing. She even created a post for women who were especially trained to carry baskets of meadowsweet in front of her at ceremonials, and to broadcast the flowers before her.

Related species are *F. ulmaria* 'Variegata' with gold splashed foliage, and *F. ulmaria* 'Aurea' with bright gold foliage. They all have cream flowers.

Mint

I shall never lack a good supply of common mint, in all its many varieties, all its colours, all its virtues. But if any man can name the full list of all the kinds and all the properties of mint, he must know how many sparks Vulcan sees fly into the air from his vast furnace beneath Etna.

Walafrid Strabo, *The Little Garden* (AD 840)

Botanical name: *Mentha*
Family: Labiatae
Other names: Mynts, mintes, myntes
Life: Perennial

Times do not change, and it is just as difficult to differentiate between various mints today as it was in the time of Walafrid Strabo. When I laid out my first nursery garden I placed four mints in close proximity to each other. Although they were divided by roof slates their roots managed to become entangled and some very strange looking mint plants developed. All mints are peripatetic and the moment they are planted they send out roots in all directions. Try to contain them and you end up with a very unhappy prisoner that needs dividing and replanting every year. They are among the easiest herbs to grow and the most difficult to control. Because there are so many variations on a theme I will list just four types, representative of their species.

ROUND-LEAFED MINT, *Mentha rotundifolia* (other names: apple mint, Bowles mint, pineapple mint,

or variegated apple mint). These are the most sweetly-scented of the mint family.

SPEARMINT, *Mentha spicata* (other names: garden mint, mackerel mint, lamb mint). There is constant argument as to whether this is the best mint to put with potatoes or not. I prefer the aromatic Bowles mint myself.

PEPPERMINT, *Mentha piperita* (other names: brandy mint). This is the mint most used by medicinal herbalists. It has dark, almost purple leaves.

PENNYROYAL, *Mentha pulegium* (other names: pudding grass, lurk-in-the-ditch). The name *pulegium* comes from the Latin 'pulex', meaning flea, as it has the reputation of deterring fleas. I use it as an ant repellent. This is a prostrate form which does well in damp shade. It likes being crushed and emits a strong smell. It is a powerful abortifacient and should never be given to pregnant women.

Myrtle

A large income is the best recipe for happiness I ever heard of. It certainly may secure all the myrtle and turkey part of it.

Jane Austen, *Mansfield Park* **(1813)**

Botanical name: *Myrtus communis*
Family: Myrtaceae
Other names: Myrte, Mirto
Life: Perennial

Myrtle is a herb that is dedicated to the protection of virgins, symbolising purity and fertility. In European countries it is often woven into a bridal wreath. There was a tradition in Tuscany of lovers giving each other a love token of myrtle. If it was not presented at each meeting the engagement was effectively ended.

Legend has it that Aphrodite was turned into a myrtle tree to disguise her from the Satyrs when she became lost in a wood. In ancient Egypt it was considered to be a powerful medicine, and Pliny claimed that the Egyptian myrtle had the most powerful scent of all. A similar claim was made some 300 years earlier about Greek myrtle by Theophrastus. It is no wonder. In a hot climate the perfume must be wonderful.

Myrtle prefers a fertile soil in full sun, and in this country, grows best in a conservatory where it can be trained against a wall. After flowering, in late summer is the best time to do this. The flowers, set off by the dark, shiny green leaves, are like the flowers of a wild rose, white or blush-pink, and give way to dark berries. The leaves are a favourite in game dishes. It is not much used in medicine these days but was traditionally used for pains of the chest and for people suffering from consumption. A toilet water, known as angel water, *eau d'ange*, can be made from myrtle, and I have recently come across a hair ointment made by Ancient Egyptians that used a red mineral, myrtle, gazelle dung and hippopotamus fat – who's going to run their fingers through that hair?

The variegated form *M. commhnis* 'Variegata' has cream blotches on the leaves which sometimes extend to the margins and form a delicate-looking border. All in all, this is a very feminine herb.

Parsley

The often use of parsley taketh away the stinking of the breath, especially from such as have drunk much wine or eaten garlike.

Richard Surflet, *The Countrie Farme* **(1600)**

Botanical name: *Petroselinum crispum*
Family: Umbelliferae
Other names: Parcely, persely, perslie
Life: Biennial

There are several superstitions attached to parsley, one being that the seed goes to the devil and back seven times before germinating. It does take a long time. But not that long. There are ways to speed up the process. One is to soak the seed overnight before sowing. The other is to pour boiling water on the seed in its drills. I prefer to let nature take its course, and sow in plug trays placed in a cold greenhouse and and checked regularly for the little green hooks to appear. The mistake often made, and I have made it myself, is to allow too many stalks to a pot, or together in the ground. Thin to at least 30 cm/12 in apart in a well cultivated soil and site where it can get some afternoon shade. It is a hungry plant and therefore needs feeding and watering well, the best time being late afternoon. Do not be tempted to denude it of leaf too soon in its development. Plants sown in spring will go to seed early the following year, so it is best sown again in late summer for a good crop next year.

Medicinally it is classed as a bitter aromatic. This points to it being a good herb for the digestion. It has been used in the treatment of cystitis, to strengthen the urinary tract and for flushing out toxins from the body. It is the next best source of iron after nettles, and is rich in vitamin C. A good restorative herb, but it should be avoided by pregnant women, although it is used to help the womb recover after birth. Parsley is also recommended as a kidney tonic.

It is well accepted as a garnish and makes a marvellous sauce. There is a plain-leafed form often called 'Italian' or 'French' parsley (*Petroselinum hortense*) which imparts a very strong flavour but is not so attractive as a garnish. A sprig of parsley really does sweeten the breath after eating garlic.

Rose

And she was fayr as is the rose in May.

Geoffrey Chaucer, *The Legend of Cleopatra*
(14th century)

Botanical name: *Rosa gallica officinalis, R. gallica versicolor, Rosa canina*
Family: Rosaceae
Other names: Apothecary rose, damask rose, dog rose
Life: Perennial

Rose oil, rose water, rose hip syrup, they all conjure up images of beauty and fragrance. The 'true' roses of herb gardens are the old roses, with pedigrees that date back to the Mogul Empire. These roses are blush-pink, red and soft white, with such delicate flowers growing on the sharpest of thorned stems. *Rosa gallica*, the 'Apothecary's' rose in Britain and some other countries, and 'Provence' rose in France, is the one most used in medicine. The dog rose, *Rosa canina* is the most nutritious. It was given its name because of its reputed ability to cure rabies. The Damask rose, *Rosa gallica versicolor,* is the most popular for making pot-pourri. It is also known as Rosa mundi. Sadly, their flowering period is short – a matter of three or four weeks in early summer. So it is best to consult an early rose specialist to mix in some of the newer Gallica introductions that have a longer flowering time. Rose petals can be gathered when dry and laid out on paper in an airy shady place and added to scented geranium leaves for a long lasting pot-pourri. They all require full sun and a well manured soil in which to thrive. One great benefit of the old scented roses is that they need no more than a light prune after flowering, and they shape quite nicely, usually covering an area of about 1.2 sq. metres/4 sq. feet.

The 'sweet eglantine' of Shakespeare's day is the 'sweet briar', smaller in leaf and flower and so called because of its sweet scent.

All the wild roses make good impenetrable hedges. Their hips,which are three times richer in vitamin than an orange, and the scent of the flowers, are nature's gift to sweeten all the senses.

Rosemary

As for Rosmary, I lett it runne all over my garden walls, not onlie because my bees love it, but because it is the herb sacred to rememberance, and, therefore, to friendship; whence a sprig of it hath a dumb language that maketh it the chosen emblem of our funeral wakes and in our buriall grounds.

Sir Thomas More, (1478–1535)

Botanical name: *Rosmarinus officinalis*
Family: *Labiatae*
Other names: Compass-weed, polar plant, incensier (Old French)
Life: Perennial

On April 23rd, Shakespeare's birthday, the people of Stratford-upon-Avon carry sprigs of rosemary in procession through the streets. This follows an old tradition that Rosemary keeps the memory green. Claudius refers to this in *Hamlet*, in his first speech of the play: 'Though yet of Hamlet our dear brother's death/The memory be green...'. The belief was, that if a sprig of rosemary was placed in the hands of the deceased it would sprout and create a fragrant bush covering the rotting corpse. Rosemary is one of the universally great herbs, and in the upright form of *R. officinalis,* develops into a splendid strong and fragrant bush displaying light blue flowers – so loved of bees – for many months of the year. Grow in a well-drained soil with plenty of grit to allow the roots to breathe. Cuttings can be taken from spring right through the year except at the height of summer. Use stems that are not in flower and place in moist sharp sand in a shady place or sow seeds in the spring. To really thrive, rosemary needs full sun and a dry soil, well sheltered, although the best bush I ever had was on a windswept allotment. Trim back soon after planting and take from it on a regular basis and it will reward you with strong new shoots and a healthy, oily leaf. Just to rub the branches of rosemary makes you feel good. Make it into a tisane to lift the spirits. Bring a flowering stem into the home to energise you. It derives its name from two words, 'ros', meaning 'dew' and 'marinus', meaning 'sea', probably because of its natural habitat along the Mediterranean coasts.

There are many types of rosemary, from the prostrate *R. officinalis* prostrate, to the delicate flowered 'Frimley Blue', and the sturdy 'Miss Jessups Upright'.

Rue

*The Weasell when she is to en-
counter the serpent arms herselfe with
eating of Rue.*

William Coles, *The Art of Simpling*
(1656)

Botanical name: *Ruta graveolens*
Family: Rutaceae
Other names: Herb of grace, herbygrass, garden rue
Life: Perennial

In recent years, Rue has become the *bête noire* of the herb garden. Members of the rue family can cause phototoxic reactions. This means that when exposed to direct sunlight the plant secretes a volatile oil which, in some people, can cause burns and blisters on the skin. Because of this it is at the top of the list of 'hazardous' plants, and should not be planted where children play or where people might be bathing. Whether or not rue has only recently developed this dangerous side to its nature, the traditional view of this most decorative herb is of healing and holiness.

Mithradates the Great, king of Pontus, used rue as the main ingredient in a antidote to poison. It was regarded as a protection against evil, and Catholic priests were supposed to have used rue as an aspergillum to anoint the congregation with holy water. This gave it the name 'herb of grace'.

In the early 18th century it was used in the infamous 'vinegar of the four thieves', (see 'Legends and Superstitions') and judges would place a sprig of rue on the bench between them and the defendant to protect them from 'gaol fever'. It is still carried, symbolically, by judges to this day on processions to the Assizes. The blue-grey, club-shaped leaves were granted as a chaplet for the heraldic device of the first duke of Saxony in 1181. This symbol later became the model for the suit of clubs in playing cards. Rue will grow to a height of 1 metre/30 in, forming a semi-evergreen woody shrub. The flowers are bright yellow and are carried in clusters on grey-green stems.
You should keep rue well away from basil: they dislike each other.
Caution: Do not use for self-medication; rather, consult a qualified medical herbalist.

76

St John's Wort

Hypericum, all bloom, so thick a swarm
Of flow'rs, like clothing her slender rods.
That scarce a leaf appears;

William Cowper, *The Task* **(1785)**

Botanical name: *Hypericum perforatum*
Family: Hypericacaea
Other names: Herb John, balm of warriors wounds, hundred holes, touch and heal, terrestrial sun
Life: Perennial

St John's wort was a favourite wound-healing herb at the time of the Crusades, but its reputation goes back even further, to Dioscorides, who in the 1st century AD compiled the *Herbarius*, detailing the sources and uses of plants.

When held up to the light you can see the oil glands in the plant's leaves, which resemble tiny holes, or perforations. The flowers are yellow, but turn the colour of blood when crushed, and, if placed in a jar with a little olive oil in full sun will yield a dark red oil. This oil is very effective against burns and wounds. The flowers and leaves have been used to treat anxiety, depression and excitability. It has been referred to as the 'arnica of the nervous system'.

St John's wort will grow well in shady places and along ditches and banks. You can divide its roots in the spring or sow seeds in seed trays. It will grow to a height of 1 metre/39 in. Flowers were traditionally gathered on St John's Day, which falls on 24 June. This herb has many legends attached to it. It was thought of as a 'magic' herb because of its healing properties. The name *Hypericum* means 'over an apparition', from the belief that it drives away evil spirits. It was regarded as a protective herb against fire and lightening. Another belief was that if a childless wife went naked to pick the flowers she would conceive within the year. Should you step on St John's wort on the Isle of Wight you would be carried off on a fairy horse, and not returned until morning.

There are a number of species in the hypericum family, but the only one closely related to St John's wort is *H. androsaemum*. Like H. perforatum it is a celebrated wound herb, but is larger and has black berries in autumn. It also prefers shade.

Sage

We count it Nature's friend and worth the having.

Sir John Harington, *The Englishman's Doctor* **(1607)**

Botanical name: *Salvia officinalis*
Family: Labiatae
Other names: Sawge, salgia, salvia ,salvatrix
Life: Perennial

Sage is a much more versatile herb than it may appear. The botanical name derives from the Latin 'salvere' meaning 'to save'. In the 16th century it has acquired a reputation for promoting long life. Thomas Coghan, in his *Haven of Health* recorded, 'As I myselfe have knowen a man of 80 yeares and upwarde, who for his breakfast in summer used to eate 6 or 7 Sage leaves minced small with a little salt...by which means he preserves himselfe long in a healthfull state.' Before this time it was recognised as one of nature's great 'cure-alls'. An old Arabian proverb says, 'How can a man die who has sage in his garden.' The Chinese were keen to give the Dutch traders three times the quantity of tea in exchange for sage leaf. In France it was looked upon as a grief herb, probably for the relief it gives to spasms in the chest region. This seems to have reached England in the 17th century when the famous diarist, Samuel Pepys, recorded seeing, 'Between Gosport and Southampton...a little churchyard where it was customary to sow all the graves with Sage.' In the war-torn coastal regions of former Yugoslavia, sage has long been a part of a thriving industry producing sage honey. In the garden the soft grey-green leaves of the common sage mix well with the dark purple leaves of red sage (*Salvia purpurea*) and variegated forms, such as 'Icterina', which are less hardy.

It grows best in full sun, in a well-drained soil. Prune well back to young shoots in late spring and take cuttings to root in sharp sand, or layer bushes in autumn. Old woody bushes can be mounded up to produce new shoots in spring. Do not be disheartened by sage's straggly appearance in winter, as it will revive in the spring, when you can remove the tips to encourage new growth below.

Salad Burnet

It has tow little leaves like unto the wings of birdes, standing out as the bird setteth her wings when she intendeth to flye. Ye Dutchmen call it Hergottes Berdlen, that is 'God's little birds', because of the colour that it hath in the topp.

William Turner, *A New Herbal* **(1551)**

Botanical name: *Sanguisorba minor*
Family: Rosaceae
Other names: *Pimpinella sanguisorba*, burnet saxifrage, lesser burnet.
Life: Perennial

This wild, unruly herb will give you sustained growth throughout the year. An easy plant to grow, it reaches a height of 40cm/15 in, with small pinnate leaves having serrated edges. The rosy coloured, globular flower heads should be cut off if you want to produce plenty of leaf. On their own the leaves do not seem to taste much, but once put into a salad or wine drink they taste of chestnut mixed with cucumber. Salad burnet makes a useful substitute herb in the winter, if you want to use fresh leaves. It is a very good herb to include in window boxes, as it fills out well providing all round interest. Keep it trimmed otherwise it gets to look a bit straggly and loses its charm. It will grow in most places in full sun or part shade and can be sown from seed in spring. If allowed to flower it will self seed freely.

Salad burnet grows in the wild all over central Europe and along the North African coast. It will be found in woodlands, and fields on dry chalk.

Related species include *Sanguisorba officinalis*, known as great burnet, which has dark green leaves and red flowers and grows to 1 metre /39 in in height. Other large forms include *S. obtusa* and *S. tenuifolia*, both of which grow to a height of 1.5 metres/5 feet. The leaves of all varieties are edible, although salad burnet has the best flavour.

Traditionally, it used as a wound healer, soldiers having used it after battle to staunch the bleeding.

Savory

Winter Savorie is altogether of like vertu with Time... Sommer Savorie is not full so hot as Winter Savorie ... it is with good success boile and eaten with beans, peason, and other windie pulses.

John Gerard, *The Herball* **(1597)**

Botanical names: *Satureia hortensis* and *Satureia montana*
Family: Labiatae
Other names: Bean herb
Life: *S. hotensis* annual; *S. montana* perennial

Winter savory (*S. montana*) makes a sweet scented edging that is a delight to brush against. In Roman times it was considered to be an aphrodisiac deriving its name from the satyrs. In Germany summer and winter savories were called 'Bohnenkraut', meaning 'bean herb', and they do indeed make a worthy addition to any bean dish. They have a similar appearance to thyme, but are more branched, with small pink or white flowers. The summer savory (*S. hortensis*) is an annual and should be sown in situ in early spring. The seeds take a long time to germinate but will produce plants for cutting by mid summer. The soil needs to be in full sun and quite rich. Thin out the seedlings to 15 cm/6 in.

Summer savory has a peppery taste and should be used sparingly. It is taller that winter savory, grow-ing to a height of 45 cm/18 in, and tends to become rather straggly. Cut it two or three times during the growing season. It is a great favourite with bees, and the leaf is said to give relief from their sting.

Summer savory is used commercially to flavour salami. Both savories have been used as moth repellents in a similar way to southernwood, placing the stems between the garments. For good strong growth, it is best to cut winter savory hard back in early spring. Although it looks dreadful for three or four weeks it benefits greatly from this cutting and produces strongly favoured leaves as a result. Most cooks prefer the summer savory, but for my part I prefer the winter savory for its scent and usefulness as a fragrant, low-growing edging herb.

Sorrel

...to quench thirst, and procure an appetite in fainting or decaying stomachs.

Nicholas Culpeper, *The English Physician*
(1653)

Botanical name: *Rumex acetosa*
Family: Polygonacaea
Other names: Green sauce, sour suds, cuckoo sorrow
Life: Perennial

The juicy stems and leaves of garden sorrel are the prime ingredients in *Soupe aux herbes,* a favourite French dish. The leaves are high in oxalic acid, which imparts a crisp, sharp taste that made this a herb reputed among country folk to quench the thirst. It likes moist, rich soil and will tolerate partial shade. Arrow-shaped, lush green leaves quickly form into large clumps developing tall flower stems of reddish-brown that grow to a height of 1 metre/3 feet. Cut the leaves on a regular basis as this helps to increase the crop.

The vitamin C content of sorrel made it a traditional remedy for scurvy. Today it is best avoided by people who suffer from gout, or kidney stones, as the crystals created by the oxalic acid can activate these symptoms.

The low-growing buckler leaf sorrel, also known as French sorrel, is lower in oxalic acid but very sharp in taste. The leaves are shield-shaped and abundant, and have small flowering stems. These should be cut off as soon as they appear to encourage more leaf growth. It makes a splendid addition to salads and is very refreshing to take on hot days in the garden.

Other related species of sorrel include broad-leaf sorrel and the silver form of buckler leaf called 'Silver Shield Leaf'. The broad leaf is a favourite of my wife's, as it puts out very little in the way of flower and grows in thick clumps. It is also a smaller variety than the common garden sorrel and is ideal for a small area. The Hopkinsons of Hollington Nurseries have developed a broad-leaf variety from rootstock which does not produce seed and grows to a height of only 30 cm/12 in. It is called 'Hollington Broad Leaf' and produces a very tender green leaf.

Southernwood

The smell of it is so strong that it will make some men's heads to ake...

Thomas Coghan, *The Haven of Health* **(1584)**

Botanical name: *Artemisia abrotanum*
Family: Compositae
Other names: Lad's love, old man, maiden's ruin, garde-robe
Life: Perennial

The feathery grey-green leaves of this decorative, aromatic shrub have been used in many ways over the centuries. It was called 'lad's love' because young boys would give a sprig of it to their girl-friends at church on Sundays. Placed in a nosegay, it also helped to sweeten the air in the often crowded congregations. The name 'old man' came about because of the grey, old beard effect it gives at the end of the season. Young boys used to rub their faces with it to promote a beard. The French gave it the name *'garde-robe'* when they used it to hang in wardrobes to deter the moth. I find it most effective for this purpose. 'Maiden's ruin' comes from the belief that it was a love charm and aphro-disiac. It has been used to treat female ailments.

The leaves and flowering tops have been used to treat delayed menstruation, threadworms in chil-dren and diseases of the scalp. This herb prefers a gritty, well drained soil in full sun, growing to a height and spread of 1 metre/39 in. At the start of the growing season in early spring, cut back to new shoots about 30 cm/12 in above the ground. It will shape into a nice hedge if you trim it in early sum-mer. Cut off the yellow flower heads. Cuttings take well in the summer and can be overwintered in the greenhouse until the spring.

Southernwood looks particularly good when planted with lavender and rosemary.

There are several varieties of artemisia, but the one most similar in look to southernwood is *Artemisia camphorata*. Like southernwood, it does not produce anything much in the way of flower, but the scent is quite different, being a heady, sweet smell of camphor, which some people find very pleasant. It makes a good herb for gardens planted for the blind.

Stinging Nettle

And thorns shall come up in her palaces, nettles and brambles in the fortresses thereof: and it shall be an habitation of dragons, and a court for owls.

Isiah: *Chap 34 vs13.*

Botanical name: *Urtica dioica*
Family: Urticaceae
Other names: Common nettle
Life: Perennial

Culpeper described stinging nettles as being, 'under the dominion of Mars', and so well known that, 'they may be found by feeling in the darkest night.' In the wild, stinging nettles are always found growing where the soil is fertile, even though it may appear to be a waste place. There is a story to illustrate this.

A blind man goes to investigate a field which he wishes to buy. On arriving at the field he asks the vendor if he might tether his donkey to the nearest clump of thistles. The vendor tells him there are no thistles. So the blind man asks if the donkey can be tied to the nearest bunch of nettles. The vendor tells him he can tie his donkey to wherever he likes as the field is full of stinging nettles. 'In that case,' says the blind man, 'I will buy your field.'

Stinging nettles invariably grow in clumps, having a similar invasive habit of mint. The leaf is very like the mint family, but they are covered in barbed hairs which contain formic acid and the resulting sting can be painful. Relief is often found from a companion plant growing nearby; the common dock. In spite of this, when cooked or placed in hot water they lose their sting and make a very good springtime tonic. The plant is a must in any medicinal garden, growing happily in sun or shade. It is a diuretic, diaphoretic (promotes sweating), expectorant and styptic. It is rich in iron and stimulates the circulation. When the Romans came to Britain they brought a giant form of stinging nettle, *Uritca pilulifera*, which they used to beat themselves with to combat the cold of the north.

The stinging nettle is a most versatile plant: it is used to make thread for tablecloths and sheets, rope and paper. The leaves make a green dye and I often use them as a compost activator.

Sweet Cicely

I use to eat them with oile and vinegar, being first boiled; which is very good for old people that are dull and without courage: it rejoiceth and comforteth the heart, and increaseth their lust and strength.

John Gerard The Herball (1597)

Botanical name: *Myrrhis odorata*
Family: Umbelliferae
Other names: Wild chervil, sweet ciss, anise fern, shepherd's needle
Life: Perennial

Sweet Cicely is a bushy, decorative herb with fern-like leaves. It grows to a height of 2 metres/6 feet. and spreads to 1 metre/39 in, making it a good backdrop plant to any border. It blends well with more solid looking upright plants such as foxglove or evening primrose. The stem is thick and ridged and the flowers, appearing in late spring or early summer, are creamy white. It has a sweet, anise scent and is much loved by bees.

The seeds should be sown in the autumn in order to germinate in frosty ground. If you do not want to plant in situ you can sow seeds in trays left outside. It has a long thick taproot, so a well cultivated rich soil helps it to grow well. Roots can be divided in spring or autumn. It may be necessary to check for self-sown seedlings as it can be quite invasive. The seeds are dark brown and grow about 5cm/1 in long.

Sweet Cicely makes a useful sugar substitute for people with diabetes, and a flavourful addition to fruit salads. It has always been considered a safe herb, and can be used freely without any fear of side effects. Traditionally it was used as a tonic for young girls during the transition from puberty to womanhood. It can be made into a warming tisane being a gentle stimulant for the stomach.

Native Americans used the whole plant, and particularly the seeds and root, in their diet. The root has also been used as a lure for horses in order to catch them.

The French like to stuff their pillows with the dried herb.

Tansy

Let those Women that desire Children love this herb, it is their best companion, their husbands excepted.

Nicholas Culpeper, *The English Physician* **(1653)**

Botanical name: *Tanacetum vulgare*
Family: Compositae
Other names: Bachelor's buttons
Life: Perennial

Tansy is a favourite gypsy herb, many name their children 'Tansy'. It is a common hedgerow plant and will grow in most soils. The flat-headed yellow flowers form a welded calyx resembling cloth buttons, and last all summer. The leaves are pungent and give off a camphor scent, which accounts for its use as an insect repellent. Housewives used to rub the meat with tansy leaves to keep off flies. In Greece it is called '*athansie*' meaning 'everlasting'. In legend, Gannymede used it to attain immortality, but it also had a darker use as a preservative for dead bodies. It is a very bitter herb and not to modern tastes, but until recently tansy cakes were eaten to end the Lenten fast. In the ancient school of medicine at Salerno, tansy was one of the six remedies recommended for palsy, although today medical herbalists would caution care in this treatment if the patient is of a nervous disposition.

But, under qualified supervision, it is a most beneficial herb. As a vermifuge, for expelling worms, for delayed periods and menstrual cramps and fevers. Externally it can be used for swellings, toothache, varicose veins, bruises, earache, styes and eye inflammation. Certainly it might have been viewed as a 'cure-all' at one time.

One word of caution: tansy, because of its ability to promote menstruation, should on no account be taken during pregnancy. This tends to contradict Nicholas Culpeper's words, but even for the sake of tradition it is not a risk worth taking. It should also not be taken for any length of time.

Tansy is invasive and grows to at least 1 metre/39 in, with a strong root system. As a companion plant it deters beetles, ants and aphis, cabbage moth. Grow it with cabbages, roses, raspberries and fruit trees and it will have a beneficial effect.

Tarragon

Tis highly cordial and friendly to the head, heart, liver, correcting the weakness of the ventricle.

John Evelyn, *Acetaria* **(1699)**

Botanical name: *Artemisia dracunculus*
Family: Compositae
Other names: Little dragon, herbe as dragon
Life: Perennial

The major difference between this French taragon and coarser Russian tarragon, *Artemisia redowski* (sometimes listed as *A. dracunculoides*), is in the form of propagation. French tarragon is a sterile plant, which, although it goes to flower, rarely sets seed. It is propagated by root division in spring or autumn, or by softwood cuttings in the summer. The roots have a similar pattern to mint and it is advisable to contain them by use of roof slates, or by placing them in a sunken container with the base removed. I find it grows best in poor, stony soil with plenty of sun. Having died down in the winter it should surface again in the spring if it has had some protection from hard frosts. A good late mulch is beneficial, or you can dig it up and bring it inside for the winter. It grows to a height of 1 metre/39 in, with woody, branching stems producing an abundance of dark green, pointed leaves.

To harvest the leaves, it is best to do so before the flowers appear round about mid summer. They should be cut very carefully so as not to bruise the leaves, which makes them kose their flavour. Dry in a dark, cool place, and use to make vinegar. Although it is a very versatile herb it is mainly used in salads and with chicken dishes. It is also the main ingredient in tartare sauce.

Although, not introduced into this country until Tudor times, it was well known as a cure for toothache by the Arabs. Its name derives from the Latin, '*dracunculus*', meaning 'little dragon', as it had a reputation for curing stings and bites from venomous reptiles.

Do try to avoid the larger cousin Russian tarragon, which grows into a large unruly bush, producing seed in abundance and having very little flavour.

Thyme

*The woods and desert caves,
With wild thyme and the gadding
vine o'ergrown.*

John Milton, *Lycidas* **(1637)**

Botanical name: *Thymus vulgaris*
Family: Labiatae
Other names: Garden thyme, common thyme
Life: Perennial

Thyme originated in the Mediterranean regions, and is one of the most savoury of all the herbs growing in the garden. It is a woody, shrub-like herb with aromatic leaves and pale purple flowers is very attractive to bees. The word '*thumus*' is Greek for 'courage', and in the days of Chivalry ladies would embroider a bee hovering over a sprig of thyme to present to their champions at the jousting tournaments. The association with magic and fairies was particularly noticeable during Shakespeare's time. In the Ashmolean Museum in Oxford there is a receipt (recipe) dated 1600 that includes thyme, which will 'Enable one to see the Fairies'.

Thyme grows very easily on stony, well drained soil in full sun. But it has the virtue of growing in any soil as long as it is not too moist. It takes well from cuttings in the summer, or you can divide plants in the spring. It is an evergreen, although it may need some protection in cold climates. A light prune in late autumn helps it to contain its strength. There are many varieties of upright and creeping thymes Creeping thymes need careful cultivation and are not as frost hardy as the uprights, but they all make wonderful edgings and scented seats.

Medicinally, thyme has been associated with the treatment of depression. The volatile oils contains thymol, a most powerful antiseptic. This has been isolated and used in cough mixtures. It also helps to relieve flatulence and soothes the digestive system. An oil made from thyme has been used to treat shingles.

Like the sages, this strong herb gives so much of itself that every four years it is best to replace it; take cuttings from the second year on for this purpose.

Wall Germander

*The decoction taken for four days driveth away
and cureth tertian and quartan agues.*

Nicholas Culpeper, *The English Physician* **(1653)**

Botanical name: *Teucrium chamaedrys*
Family: Labiatae
Other names: Common germander, hedge germander, petit chêne
Life: Perennial

Wall germander reaches a height of only 45 cm/18 in, with small green, oak-shaped, toothed leaves on branching woody stems. If it is clipped into shape before flowering it makes an ideal low border hedge, very similar to buxus, but infinitely cheaper. It also grows more quickly. If grown as a border plant the flowers appear for at least two months in summer; they are rose pink. Seeds can be sown in the spring, and cuttings taken in the summer. You can divide plants in autumn.

Wall germander grows well in a good loamy soil, with a small addition of grit or shingle. I have grown it as a low barrel-shaped hedge surrounding my front garden and although it only gets sun in the morning and early afternoon it has done very well. Wall Germander was traditionally used for gout, Emperor Charles V having been a grateful patient. Nicholas Culpeper recommended it for

ulcers, tired eyes, pains in the side and cramps. He also suggests that it might have been effective for reviving the vital spirit. Its constitutents include an essential oil, and it has antiseptic, astrigent and bitter tonic properties, among others. Today it is mostly used for the treatment of osteoarthritis and can be used externally to treat slow-healing wounds and haemorrhoids.

Wall germander is native to southern and central Europe, where it grows in woodland, on dry, sunny banks, on rocks and walls. It was introduced to Britain as a medicinal herb and is now widely cultivated, although it can sometimes be found growing on old walls, where it has become naturalised. A related species, *Teucrium scordodonia*, or wood sage, is native to Britain. This has sage-like leaves with yellow flowers, and, as its name implies, grows well in shady places under trees.

Woodruff

Hanged up in houses, it doth very well attemper the aire, coole and make fresh the place to the delight and comfort of such as are therein.

John Gerard, *The Herball* **(1597)**

Botanical name: *Galium odoratum*
Family: Rubiaceae
Other names: Sweet Woodruff, muge-de-boys
Life: Perennial

Woodruff is a late spring-flowering, shade-loving herb that, as its name implies, grows in woodland. The dark green leaves encircle the square stems at even intervals, and resemble Elizabethan ruffs. When brought into the house and dried, it has the intoxicating scent of new-mown hay. As a result it was a strewing herb, and was also used to stuff mattresses and to perfume bed linen. In Germany it is steeped in white wine and made into a May Day drink known as *Maibowle*.

Woodruff can be divided in the spring when it first appears after the winter, and roots can be taken for most of the year. This herb is a marvellous spreading plant and seems to double its size each year. In spring the tiny white flowers appear to float above the ruffs, and look wonderful en masse. Medicinally, woodruff is a favourite with gypsies, who make it into a tea. It has been used to increase milk flow in young mothers, and also has a nervine effect. Woodruff has proved to be helpful in the treatment of such diverse conditions as constipation, forgetfulness, jaundice and hysterial, and for reducing feverishness. However, this is not a herb to take too much of, and a decent interval between treatments is advised.

Related species include *Galium verum,* known as 'lady's bedstraw', which is a much taller, more ragged herb with yellow flowers, and *Asperula tinctoria,* known as 'dyer's woodruff'. Both of these have been used for dyeing.

Wormwood

Botanical name: *Artemisia absinthium*
Family: Compositae
Other names: Green ginger, absinth, St John's girdle
Life: Perennial

Taking its name from its ability to expel worms, this aromatic, silver-leafed herb is a powerful bitter. Wormwood was introduced into this country in 1548 and became a 'monastic' herb, probably as a result of the legend that St John the Baptist wore a girdle of wormwood about his waist. It is not, however, accepted that the wormwood we know today is that which is mentioned in the bible. Traditionally, it was looked upon as a herb for women's ailments and classed with the other artemisias. It was used to promote menstruation, and as a tonic before and after childbirth. Today, its ability to restore the appetite has meant that it has been used in cases of anorexia nervosa. But it has a down side too. Its bitter principle is absinthum, which went into the flavouring of the French drink, absinthe. This was found to be addictive and to have a destructive effect on the central nervous system, in severe cases causing epileptic fits. Taken as a tea it can have quite alarming hallucinogenic properties, as indeed its sister plant, 'mugwort' (*Artemisia vulgaris*), also has. Treated with respect and taken in small doses, wormwood is an excellent digestive bitter tonic, but I would always advise seeking qualified medical help before attempting any self treatment.

I find it grows well in the garden in sun, or shade, although it prefers a shady position. As it grows to a height of 1.2 metres/4 feet, it should be placed towards the back of a border. The small clusters of yellow flowers in late summer are insignificant. It is best propagated by root division, in spring, otherwise take softwood cuttings in early summer. Dried, it makes a good moth repellent and you can infuse it for use as an insecticide. It is not a good companion to roses.

Yarrow

Yarroway, Yarroway, bear a white blow,
If my love love me, my nose will bleed now.

East Anglian Rhyme.

Botanical name: *Achillea millefolium*
Family: Compositae
Other names: Soldier's woundwort, herbe militaris, nose bleed. carpenter's weed, yarroway
Life: Perennial

The finely divided grey-green leaves of yarrow led William Coles, in his *Doctrine of Signatures*, to believe that this was a herb which should help in blood disorders, because of the appearance of the leaf, which resembles a network of veins. Although William Coles's theory has now been discredited, yarrow has always had a reputation as a styptic, and today is used by medical herbalists to dissolve clots in thrombosis, for the treatment of varicose veins and piles. I once cut myself quite badly with a pair of secateurs and, with no sticking plaster in sight, wrapped the wound with yarrow leaves. Crushed, to release the oil, and applied, tied about with twine, I was amazed at the speed with which the flow of blood was stemmed and the wound healed perfectly. Evidence of the antiseptic quality was clear, as I failed to get any infection in the soil-covered cut. Perhaps I was lucky, but it

certainly led me to believe in the legend of Achilles healing his soldiers' wounds on the field of battle with yarrow. Its name derives from this ancient hero and the word 'milfoil', meaning 'thousand-leafed'. Yarrow staunches nose bleeds, but also promotes them if rubbed in the nostrils. It was used as a cure for headache; also a masochistic 'love charm' if the rhyme above was taken seriously.

I grow yarrow mostly for its ability to inhabit rough places, although the flat heads of tiny white flowers are quite attractive, even though it has a straggly appearance – it grows to a height of 60 cm/24 in. As a flu and cold tonic, yarrow, elder-flower and peppermint in equal parts, taken every two hours, takes away much of the discomfort. At least from personal experience I can vouch for it being a fever herb and a wound herb. For the headaches, I think I'll stick to peppermint tea.

Creating a Herb Garden

There is no mystery to creating a herb garden. But there are a few hard and fast rules that will enable you to be successful in your project. Site, sun and well prepared soil are the three most important things to remember. That scrubby bit of badly drained yard at the shady side of the house is not the best place to site a herb garden, in spite of its convenient location. Herbs may sometimes look like weeds but even weeds require some light, and soil that isn't wet and compacted. Look around for that area where the sun shines for at least five hours a day and you will be on your way to finding a good home for your herbs.

We can't all have the perfect soil, but we can improve on what we have, and it doesn't take an awful lot of preparation to do so. Even heavy clay can be made to suit some herbs and in small gardens structures such as a herb spiral can use imported soil.

The site will depend upon the style of your garden. But always be aware of the need to protect the garden

This is a fine example of the Victorian-style potager. The carefully planted herbs and vegetables allow for easy identification and access for harvesting. Formal beds with wide gravel paths give a sense of order to what might otherwise be a difficult garden to maintain.

from high winds and to trap as much sun as possible. Later I shall suggest different types and varieties of hedges and boundary walls and fences. All of these go to making your garden a more interesting place in which to be. Herb gardens should be places to linger in, so benches, seats, arbours and pergolas have an important role to play. You can make turf benches, chamomile seats, rose-covered arbours and covered pergolas to walk through.

The paths can be used as scented walkways or simply as a means of getting from one part of the garden to another, but they must fit in with the general scheme of things and not upset the balance of the design. A pathway needs to be functional but must not detract from the overall effect. Never underestimate the need for easy access to herb borders.

Features such as statuary, urns and pots, and topiary can enhance your herb garden, sometimes offering that final touch that makes it individual to you. The decision on what to include is very often an impulsive one inspired by a dream rather than by a planned idea, although sometimes, too, the object is a long neglected relic that has lain for years waiting for its moment to be resurrected and given pride of place again. One of my favourite seats was one such lost relic, its iron supports left lying where the rotten wooden slats had let them fall, like dead book-ends. With a coat of paint and new slats it made a very comfortable seat again.

Finally, let your imagination run away with you a little on paper so that you retain a wish yet to be fulfilled for the future. This will keep the garden alive for you as each year goes by.

Choosing your site

You may have already done this before making your plan. If you have, then take the plan to the site and mark out with wooden pegs where the main corners are and see if the alignment is right. By 'pegging out' you can tell immediately if your plan is going to translate successfully or not.

If you haven't made a plan yet but want to put your herb garden in a particular place; perhaps near to the kitchen, or tucked away somewhere, then go to the site and check for the important requirements for good results.

Does it get enough sunshine? Five hours is the minimum requirement for good results.

Is there any shade from neighbouring buildings, trees or large shrubs? If there is, can this be incorporated into your design? Obviously a formal garden needs an open setting. But less formal ones can benefit from some shade, particularly if you are growing medicinal herbs, for instance.

Is the soil of reasonable quality, not too dry or too wet? Is it clay or chalk, heavy or light? The presence of nettles can denote good soil, whereas thistles can indicate the need for improving the content.

Will you need to put in hedging or other forms of boundary? After preparing the site this is usually the first job you need to do.

Having satisfied these main criteria then you are ready to take a spade to the soil and begin the preparation for your herb garden.

An antique terracotta urn lifts the eye away from the low-growing *Geranium macrorrhizum* and introduces an architectural feature to the herb garden. For additional interest the urn might be planted in the summer with a scented geranium such as 'Lady Plymouth'.

Preparing the site

Herbs like a well aerated soil, allowing their roots to spread easily, and this is best achieved by making the soil crumble and slightly gritty. It doesn't need to be richly fed as this can make plants weaker and impair their scent. Most plants have originated in the wild and are used to quite rough ground, so don't feel you need to pamper them.

After turning over the soil you will have a good idea whether you have a light or heavy consistency. Drainage is the most important feature and if your soil is heavy, wet clay then you will have to spend some time incorporating manure and pea shingle with some sharp sand to help break it up and allow your herb roots to breathe. If the soil is very heavy and will take years to break down then consider creating a herb spiral or growing on raised beds and banks using imported loam mixed with grit. With all the herb gardens I have worked upon I have found that, with the introduction of pea shingle and a little sharp sand, the growth rate has been enhanced and the herbs have

flourished. Manure and compost do help to improve the soil but only add well rotted manure, and apply compost sparingly. I am very fortunate to have a well-balanced soil with plenty of natural grit, as it used to be a river bed, and it therefore drains well too. But every now and then I help it along with a light feed. If you don't have any compost or manure use a little bone meal, which you can buy from the garden centre.

In the impoverished chalk soil of some downland areas the topsoil is minimal as the depth of soil is often limited to only a few centimetres. Raised beds with plenty of mulch, such as homemade compost, can be the answer here. Flints and chalk will always work their way to the surface and the topsoil can dry out very quickly. Do not hope for too neat a garden but do not be deterred by this unforgiving soil; many herbs of the mint, or Labiatae family do quite well in chalk. Examples are: catnip, hyssop, marjoram, rosemary, salad burnet and sage.

Left: A shady herb border including comfrey, sweet woodruff and sorrel is fronted by cotton lavender, which will require clipping if it is to be used as a formal edging. **Below:** Various flowering upright thymes soften the otherwise severe edge of the lawn in this sunny herb border, which has yet to be planted out with summer annuals.

If your soil is a heavy acid soil then you will need to add some limestone in order to break it down. Only a small quantity is needed and it is best applied in the autumn. If you wish to add manure then wait a while to allow the limestone to work its way in first.

Having then forked over the site you should now be ready to plant your hedges, or erect your boundary fences or walls.

Walls and fences

A walled garden is something most of us only dream about. The protection offered and the reflected heat makes a wall an ideal boundary for any herb garden. All the Victorian kitchen gardens for large estates were walled gardens and some still remain. But for us lesser mortals we have to use alternative forms of protection for our plants.

A warm red-brick wall offers shelter for Comfrey grandiflorum, contrasting well with the cut-leaf gold elder 'Sutherland's Gold'.

The idea of an enclosed garden isn't something new. It dates back centuries, and many of the old ideas are relevant today. Interwoven wattle fencing secured to stout posts with wire makes an excellent low boundary and climbers can find easy ways to spread among the weave. Again, it's the immediate 'old' look that wattle gives which is so attractive.

A low drystone wall can make a useful boundary, allowing you to transform a slope and offer another dimension to the garden. At my first nursery I set a chamomile seat back into a bank, with a drystone wall at either side. Lemon thyme and winter savory with dwarf forms of lavender and hyssop grew happily around the seat. There was enough shade at the foot of the wall to grow Corsican mint and pennyroyal.

Any form of strong wooden fence will support a hop or honeysuckle. Wires can be fixed horizontally to allow for tying in of roses or as a support for hops or clematis. Openwork fencing is often very effective when you can see the herb garden through it which adds to the effect of an enclosed space.

Tall plants such as angelica, fennel and lovage benefit tremendously from having a backdrop, so it is worth bearing this in mind when creating your boundary. The most important thing to bear in mind is the need for maximum light, so plan the height of your boundaries in keeping with the size of garden.

Paths and paving

Once you have established your boundary then comes the task of 'pegging out' the outline of beds and pathways. This gives you a very precise idea as to how much room you have for edgings and low hedges.

Place pegs of wood at all the corners and tie string between them. Inevitably you are going to compact the soil doing this, so try to mark out your pathways first and lay down boards if you have them.

You will by now have decided on what sort of path you are going to have, but in all cases it is advisable to set a good base of rough rubble or hoggin below a level of sharp sand before laying your bricks or paving.

Above left: Prostrate rosemary in Provence cascading over a drystone wall enclosing a terraced bed. **Below:** Brick edging set into concrete acts as a secure border for well-firmed gravel paths. The wattle fence provides a perfect support for a honeysuckle or wild briar rose.

Gravel paths should also have a well broken base of rubble to keep the gravel from sinking into the earth. The better you prepare the rough material the less shingle you require, and you won't end up with a good imitation of a shingle beach, which you have to wade through ankle deep.

In order to enclose and encase your path it is a good idea to set gravel board at the edges, held in by wooden pegs. This is the method I use for what I call a 'living' path, set on sharp sand to allow creeping herbs to be grown in the cracks. This is an altogether pleasing path to make and soon gives the feeling of having been there for a long time. The more permanent path, a favourite with builders, is edged with bricks set on end in a cement mix. However, it can be edged on the garden side with board to allow plants to be grown as close to the path as possible. The average width of a path is either 90cm/39in or 1.2m/4 feet for small gardens, although one wide central walkway is more suitable for some designs.

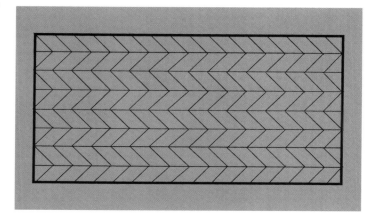

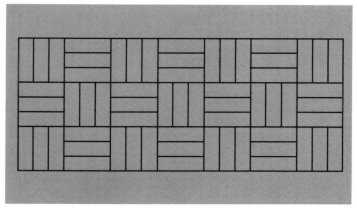

Above right and right: Simple herringbone and basketweave patterns for brick paths should be set in sharp sand to allow for planting between the cracks. **Below:** Concrete paving can be relieved by the addition of brick as shown here; it soon loses its harshness by the introduction of hedging plants such as buxus. Gravel provides contrasting texture.

If you can get old bricks, do so. You will always be told of the risk of flaking and cracking up in the frost, but this all adds to the old effect that works so well in herb gardens. The simplest patterns in brick are the best. Tudor pattern, or 'basketweave', and 'herringbone' are the easiest to lay.

Once you have set your bricks then brush in a mixture of sharp sand and soil into the cracks and sprinkle over with water. This helps to consolidate the mixture and sets the path. Keep adding this mix until the cracks are all filled. Then brush off all the bricks when dry with a stiff brush. If the path is a long one use a spirit level to keep it even, and put boards between the pegs to check your levels.

You can equally well set out stepping stones in soil mixed with gravel in order to plant out a thyme walk. Although this takes a while to establish it makes a very delicate pathway.

Paving stones and cobble stones make good courtyards, allowing for sufficient space in between slabs at varying intervals to plant out herbs. The most effective courtyards are those where herbs have self sown between the cracks and there is a sense of organised chaos about the place.

Above left: Chamomile helps to break up a paved area that includes unusual containers. **Above:** Small irregular-shaped herb beds are enclosed by a mixture of brick and paving. **Left:** A formal box hedge opposite informal edging plants. The White Rose of York, *Rosa alba semiplena*, climbs the old brick wall. **Opposite:** Copper-coloured dwarf berberis and grey-green cotton lavender provide a striking contrast in this hedge border, which includes *Salix helvetica* grown as standards.

If you plan on using lawn or chamomile for your paths then it is vital you plant out border plants or low hedges to help define the herb beds.

Hedges and edging

Herb hedges are the bones of the garden skeleton. Once you have supplied the structure then you fill in the flesh of the herb beds.

All the hedging plants most suited to edges are shrubby aromatic herbs and evergreens. They can be clipped and cut to shape and have a long lifespan. I have tried rock hyssop as a hedging plant, and although it was highly recommended to me I have found it fails on two counts: it is only semi-evergreen and it needs replacing after four or five years. You need a hedge that will last and look good in the winter months as well. The dark black, leaf-denuded stems of poor old rock hyssop do not make a pleasing sight in the early spring.

My favourites for hedging are: santolina, wall germander, lavender, rosemary and curry plant. The best of all, however, is buxus, or box to give it its common name.

Box hedging is the most formal of herb edgings. It can be trimmed into neat, straight-sided hedges anything up to 1 metre/3 feet in height. There are dwarf varieties which can be set 10–12 cm/4–5 in apart for an instant hedge. The larger *Buxus sempervirens* needs at least 30 cm/12 in between plants to establish a thick hedge over three years. Nothing happens overnight in a garden and you will need some patience with box before you achieve the smooth, manicured lines of an established garden hedge. When choosing your box plants go to a specialist grower who can advise you on the best varieties. There are in fact over 40 different types of box, although the main ones are *B. sempervirens*, *B. rotundifolia* and the dwarf, *B. suffruticosa*. Although box likes moisture it still needs a well aerated soil with the addition of a little leaf mould and peat

Hard brick edges contrast with the soft lavenders and erect alliums to provide pleasing borders, with tall hedges and ivy-covered trellis giving shelter from winds and frost. The enclosed nature of such a garden retains heat and scent and encourages visits from butterflies and bees. Shelter and sunlight help to make this a garden of abundant growth.

when planting out. Feed plants in the early spring and don't prune until the frosts are well past in early summer. This allows the new leaf growth to harden off well in time for next winter. Light clipping is possible throughout the summer.

Santolina, or cotton lavender, is particularly effective as an edge for grass paths. The contrast in its light grey colour and the green of the grass makes the hedging stand out and highlights the differences in texture. Cotton lavender can be clipped into straight-sided edges with a flat top in the late spring, and if it gets out of hand one season then cut it quite hard back in the spring to just above the new growth on lower stems.

Wall germander, which I call poor man's box, makes a good low hedge that can be trimmed into a barrel shape for best effect. The leaves are quite dark.

This herb grows on quite quickly and should be set at 10 cm/4 in apart to create a thick hedge within two years. As with all hedging herbs, do not allow it to flower if you want a good hedge, so trim regularly.

Lavender and curry plant are less easy to shape as they grow in a naturally round habit. Any heavy pruning should be left till the spring and even then you should be careful not to cut back into old wood. It seems a crime not to let lavender flower, so harvest the stalks in late summer and cut all dead stalks off before the winter. But do leave shaping until the following year. All hedging plants can be reared from cuttings, and it is not a bad idea to keep some back in case of loss to any part of the hedge. Then you will have a plant at the same stage of growth with which to replace it. Find another part of the garden where you can keep these stock plants safely.

The upright forms of Rosemary such as *officinalis* and 'Mrs Jessup's Upright' are particularly suited to large hedges but they do need a sheltered sight to avoid frosting. I have seen some rosemarys clipped savagely

but appearing to suffer little from this and looking very strong and elegant. They can be trimmed throughout the summer but should be left well alone before the first frosts are likely to occur.

In my early experimental days of herb growing I tried rue, hyssop, sage and southernwood as low hedges but found none of them to be satisfactory. You must be able to clip your hedges, and a year-round leaf growth is vital to the whole look of the garden.

Around sunny salad beds a border of chives or garlic works well. Double-flowering chamomile, lady's mantle, winter savory, catmint and dwarf dianthus such as 'Deltoides' have all been used as edging plants by me. The chives are lovely when in flower but look a bit ragged later on, but winter savory gives off the most marvellous scent when you brush past it that it has to be my favourite.

For mixed vegetable and herb gardens, bricks set at an angle give a neat appearance to the beds and rope terracotta tiles can be quite attractive too.

Above: Mass plantings of evergreen herbs in these formal semi-circular beds give a solid structure to the design. **Left:** Cotton lavender makes a show of colour when in flower, although the pungent scent is not to everyone's liking. It has an added disadvantage: the weight of the flowers opens up the centre of the shrub. **Below:** Shapes for hedging herbs, some of which are suitable for topiary.

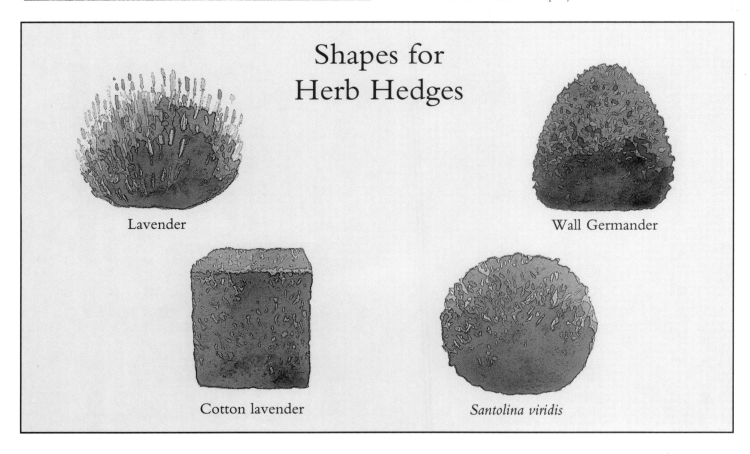

Shapes for Herb Hedges

Lavender

Wall Germander

Cotton lavender

Santolina viridis

Seats and arbours

Earth benches were a great favourite with medieval gardeners. They were often brick walls surrounding the garden, with turf laid on the top. This has given way in modern times to the chamomile seat, of which many types can be made. The easiest type to construct is one that is set into a steep bank, as it is not going to be much more than 45 cm/18 in high unless you have your feet dangling in the air. You can build up the front with dry stone and set bricks behind into the soil to create the other three sides. The seat needs to be at least 50 cm/20 in deep. Make sure the soil drains well and plant out the centre with lawn chamomile, 'Treneague', or Roman chamomile. If you want a more solid construction then build a bench surround-ed with brick and put plenty of stone and broken

Right: Mature honeysuckle provides shade for a garden seat placed underneath a wooden pergola. Pergolas can be planted with a variety of climbing plants – hop, clematis and roses are ideal. **Below:** A decorative seat surrounded by scented herbs such as dianthus 'Doris', Roman chamomile and hyssop. **Opposite:** A rose-covered pergola with catmint borders creates a scented walk within a spacious garden.

Above: A delicate painted steel arbour incorporating a seat in a small London garden is enhanced by the golden hop behind. **Above right:** A simple wooden pergola with climbing rose, hop and entwining ivies.

crock at the base to assist drainage. Then fill the cavity with earth and plant your herb. You can also try railway sleepers or fill in an old stone seat after removing the top. This type of seat can be planted with low-growing thymes as well; both make soft, sweet-scented places to sit. But do watch out during the flowering season: bees do not take at all kindly to being sat upon.

All herb gardens benefit from a seat of one sort or another. You can surround them with sweet-smelling herbs such as lavender, artemisias such as southern-wood, pinks and tender perennials such as pineapple sage and lemon verbena; and you can surround yourself above as well with a shady arbour.

Arbours can serve two main functions; either to conceal the occupant of the seat or to contain the heat of the sun and the scents around you. The view is important, so place your seat where you are going to get the maximum benefit. It is sometimes a good idea to place it directly opposite the entrance to the herb garden so that you can watch for visitors and also make it a focal point. Or you could hide it away in a sunny

corner so that it comes as a surprise and offers seclusion as well.

The construction can be quite rustic or as formal as a wrought iron surround. Wooden poles set well into the ground may rot in time but once covered in honeysuckle or jasmine can soon be submerged in scented growth. There are some semi-evergreen honeysuckles, but do make sure they are scented before buying. A briar rose or small flowering climber can be very evocative of the Elizabethan age when it seems everywhere was covered in roses.

Golden hop is quite stunning during the summer and is bold enough to grow over a large pergola. Although hop dies down in the early winter once it has produced its heady scented flower cones, it comes again even more strongly the following spring. I don't think clematis should be discounted either just because it's no longer classed as a herb. In particular the clematis 'Tangutica' grows rampantly and produces yellow bells in late summer that last well into autumn.

Pergolas are in effect arbours to walk through; as such they can be planted in a similar way. But always think of the view on either side and do not block it out, otherwise you will lose the pleasure that is part of the covered walkway.

Lawns and herb banks

To tread on the apple- scented cushion that goes by the name of a chamomile lawn is quite an experience; and if you know how many hours of painstaking work it took to create it you certainly feel you deserve to be delighted. A chamomile lawn conjures up an image of sweet-scented rolling swards of pleasure, but do not be fooled into thinking you can maintain a lawn the size of a tennis court. Think more in terms of a large carpet and then you won't be disappointed.

Start with a small area and then expand into the full area of about 6 sq. metres/64 sq. ft when you have tested the growth potential. If you have a seat at one end of the lawn then begin your herb lawn around that. Prepare the soil as if you were going to sow a seeded lawn. Remove all weeds and rake the stones off the surface. Tread or roll well and add a little bone meal or fertiliser and leave for a week or two. If the soil is heavy then add a little sharp sand before you roll it. Plant established chamomile 'Treneague' – or *Anthemis*

nobilis if you want flower – quite close together in a criss-cross pattern. For quicker results plant no more than 10 cm/4 in apart. It will take at least two seasons before you have a decent cushion of chamomile to walk on, and you must remove all weeds before they become established. Chamomile spreads from its centre and often dies down at the centre having sent out its runners. So be prepared to fill in these gaps with some of the offshoots as and when they appear. 'Treneague' needs no more than a very light trim in the summer, but the Roman chamomile *Anthemis nobilis* will need to be cut with shears on a regular basis during the growing season. But do not be downhearted by the threat of high maintenance. Once established, you will only have to keep an eye out for rogue weeds. If you have the time and patience you can create a lush green carpet to give you pleasure all summer.

Paths leading to a focal point, such as this distant fountain at Hollington Herb Nursery in Berkshire, can take you through a variety of carefully graded herbs which move from low-growing forms to tall background plants, thereby creating a valley of interest.

You can also make lawns from creeping thymes using the same technique, although I like to put plenty of grit at the surface to allow the plants to grip onto something as they spread their rooting stems outwards. You can create patterns with the different colours and allow for some to follow on from others in the flowering season. Thyme is also useful for filling in gaps that often occur in a chamomile lawn.

I had a herb garden once with quite a steep bank which was south-facing and had a variety of light and shade, the result of a large bay tree on my side and the neighbour's trees on the other side. I was amazed by the angelica which grew at the top of the bank; it was so large it gave the impression of a tree. Comfrey grew in the shade of the bay tree with woodruff and foxgloves on the other side in the shade of the trees. However, it also struck me that not all the herbs did well on that bank and it was some time before I realised that drainage was the problem. If you consider that dry herbs can grow at the top of the bank while moisture-loving herbs such as chives need to go to the bottom, then you begin to create something like a wild habitat, where St John's wort, alpine strawberry and cowslips find their own growing areas. By moving them around I began to discover their natural needs, and so it was that I came to discover the herb spiral.

Above right: Early morning sunlight highlights the leaves of lady's mantle, aconite and golden marjoram on this gently sloping bank.
Below: A chamomile lawn doesn't have to be a dream: even if you only have a hard surface, by removing a few bricks or slabs anyone can enjoy the delicate apple-scented aroma of this calming herb, which delights in being trodden upon.

The herb spiral

In order to make as near perfect an 'eco-system' for culinary herbs as possible, the science of permaculture has devised the 'herb spiral'. Permaculture is an environmentally friendly system using improvisation and the resources available to develop organic ways of cultivation. If herbs are given their natural environment they will be more resistant to pest and disease and need little help from artificial feeds and additives. The herb spiral creates the best drainage and light principles for a variety of culinary herbs, so providing a suitable herb garden that requires the minimum maintenance and yet gives the maximum yield. Plants at the top of the spiral are in drier soil than those at the bottom. So herbs such as rosemary can get the most light with less moisture, whereas mint and chives can gain shade from the walls and mositure at the bottom of the spiral. Watering can be carried out from the top and run down to the damper parts below. If you also consider that it only takes up an area about 1.5 metres/5 feet across and less than 100 cm/39 in high it is an ideal small garden to place near the kitchen. It can be constructed with around 100 bricks or dry stone walling and is remarkably easy to build. If you wish you can place a small plastic-lined pool at the base in which to grow watercress.

A Herb Spiral

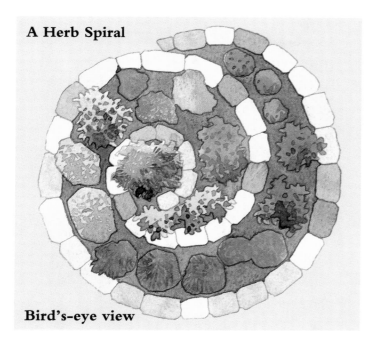

Bird's-eye view

A Herb Spiral

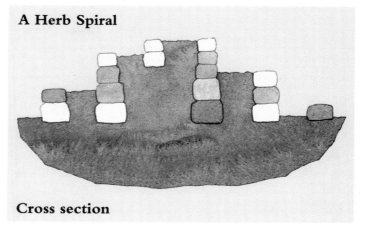

Cross section

The herb spiral displays all your culinary herbs in a helter-skelter arrangement, offering ideal light, shade and drainage conditions. Bricks or slabs can be set in a spiralling pattern without any need for mortar or cement. Rosemary, which prefers dry conditions, can be planted at the top and moisture-loving herbs such as chives and garlic at the bottom.

Growing Herbs

erbs are grown in three different ways: from seed, from cuttings and by root division. All these methods are easy to do; you need only follow a few simple guidelines to achieve success. You can help yourself enormously by using the right equipment as this will maximise your results. There are some excellent proprietary composts on the market for seeds and seedlings and you can also make up your own mix if you so wish. Here then is a list of items you need for propagating:

Having everything to hand before sowing seed or taking cuttings makes life so much easier. An ordered system of work makes for more relaxed and therefore efficient propagation. Here the materials and equipment needed for sowing have been collected together.

- Seed or plug trays
- A garden sieve
- A small dibber (for making holes)
- A good sharp knife (for cutting holes)
- Plant labels
- Indelible pens, or pencil
- Potting tray
- Glass to cover seeds
- Good quality compost for seeds and cuttings
- Small pots for seedlings and cuttings
- Spray or watering can with fine rose
- Hormone rooting compound

Growing from seed

Generally, herbs grown from seed tend to be annuals or biennials. However, there are some perennials such as chives, marjoram and thyme that can be grown from seed, although they do seem to take a long time.

Spring is the busiest seed-sowing season for chervil, dill, catmint, borage, chamomile, fennel, hyssop, lemon balm, marjoram, meadowsweet, parsley, rocket, salad burnet, summer savory and thymes. I like to wait until the warm days of late spring before sowing basil and coriander.

Spring sowings can be done in seed trays and started off indoors under glass. The ideal place, of course, is a greenhouse, although a sunny window sill, an airing

Young parsley, and even youger basil, have been grown from seed in the author's greenhouse. A greenhouse is an ideal place for raising plants from seed, but a sunny windowsill or airing cupboard will do as just as well for most herbs. By using plug trays the young seedlings can easily be potted on without causing undue distress to their root systems. The alternative is to use an ordinary seed tray or small pots.

cupboard or conservatory will do just as well in the early stages. But do make certain you keep a constant eye on your sowings at all times.

Either fill a seed tray or plug tray with seed compost. Plug trays are much easier to get now, and give you the chance to produce rooted seedlings separated from each other and therefore less likely to suffer from root disturbance when potted on. Seed compost can be bought ready mixed or you can make your own with a mix of peat and sharp sand, in a ratio of 70 per cent peat to 30 per cent sand. Or you can mix equal portions of peat and well composted forest bark. If you are unhappy about using peat, then there are some good peat substitutes, for example coir fibre, but I find they tend to dry out rather more quickly. If peat comes from a well-managed peat bog, then there is no reason why the land should be depleted. There have been, in addition, large tracts of peat bog discovered in Russia, and peat from there is being exported world-wide. Another method is to use ordinary garden soil, sterilise it and then mix it with some sharp sand.

Gently firm the compost down. In a seed tray, you can use the base of a flower pot to do this; with a plug tray you can tap the whole tray down on an even surface. This will settle the compost in the compartments. Sow your seeds thinly and lightly cover with some sieved compost. If your seeds are very small, only use a light covering. Water with a fine rose, but only just enough to dampen the soil: you don't want to soak the compost completely.

Cover the seed trays with glass to keep in the moisture and place newspaper over the glass to exclude the light while the seeds germinate. Some seed trays come with a clear lid, in which case you need only cover this with newspaper.

Put your trays in a warm place to bring the seeds on. Cover with a sheet of glass and place a piece of newspaper on top to keep out the light. Germination can take as little as five days or, in the case of parsley, anything up to two or three weeks, so keep checking the trays daily for moisture retention and the first sign of the seedlings appearing. As soon as the seedlings show, remove the glass and the newspaper and place in a light and airy place so that you encourage strong, straight seedlings to develop.

Pricking out

If you are using plug trays you will need to reduce the seedlings to one per plug. If you are using seed trays you will have to 'prick out' the overcrowded young seedlings, taking care to moisten the soil first and isolate each chosen seedling without disturbing its roots. This is a labour of love. But when you have divided all your seedlings into neat, well separated rows it is very satisfying. Give yourself plenty of time to do this task and all will be well.

If the danger of heavy frosts has passed and the soil is easily worked into a fine tilth, then you can sow seeds outdoors. Rake the soil well and make a shallow drill with a stick or edge of the rake. Moisten the bottom of the drill and sow the seeds thinly. Lightly cover the seeds with soil and then cover with a cloche, if you have one. Don't worry if you haven't, the seeds will just take a little longer to germinate.

Always mark your rows clearly with indelible pen on a good-sized label. Even with your seed trays it helps to mark them in some way in case you get into a muddle after sowing.

Keep seedlings moist with a fine spray but be careful not to overwater at this early stage. Keep a watch at this time of the year for the plants that have self-seeded from last season. Dill, borage, feverfew, parsley, fennel and chervil are all self-seeders.

Growing on

Once your seedlings have made a good root system then you can pot them on. With plugs this is a relatively easy process, but either way you need to be patient and careful in your task. Having first watered your seedlings well, you then prise them gently out of the compost and transplant them into a potting compost mixture.

Fill your flower pots in advance. Small pots are best at this stage, as this allows the roots to hit the sides of the pots quickly and so develop a strong root system. You can buy very good multi-purpose potting composts or make your own mix, remembering to include a fertiliser and vermiculite to help aerate the soil. In all good mixes you need loam, peat, grit, vermiculite, sharp sand and fertiliser. You can use short- or long-term fertilisers, but if you use short term ones you will need to add a liquid feed after 12 weeks.

Using your dibber, make a hole large enough to take the seedling, and, lifting by a leaf, gently place the seedling into the pot and firm lightly around it. It is necessary to avoid picking up seedlings by their stems as this can damage the plant and retard its growth.

I like to grow my young seedlings in the greenhouse to begin with. You can use a sunny windowsill if you don't have a greenhouse, but keep turning the plant to encourage it to grow straight up. All-round light guarantees a straight strong young plant. I place the pots on pea shingle to allow them to drain easily, but there are many forms of water-absorbing matting to put on greenhouse shelves, which help to retain moisture at the roots. Watering is important at this stage. Young plants need moisture on a regular basis, but do not like getting their feet too wet. If you water from above and use a spray mist for the leaves this will provide all the moisture they need.

After two or three weeks you will need to harden the young plants off. Take them from the greenhouse as the days warm up and put them in a sheltered, airy place, continue to water and, if necessary, feed lightly. You will notice them strengthen quite quickly and very soon they will be ready to plant out in the garden.

At the planting out stage herbs can look quite small, so check the size and spread of your plants beforehand.

Make sure the soil is well turned and able to drain freely. Water in the young plants using a watering can with a fine rose spray attachment, and then simply wait for them to grow. You will be surprised at just how quickly they come along.

The greenhouse is ideal for housing a selection of herbs which have been potted on. These plants are now strong enough to be taken from the greenhouse and hardened off outside. The process of potting on is essential for establishing a strong root system, one that is capable of producing a strong, mature plant.

Root division

Root division serves two important functions. It is an easy way to increase herbs such as chives and comfrey, and it helps to check the invasiveness of prolific spreading herbs such as mint.

With thick-rooted plants, for example comfrey and lovage, it is necessary to use a sharp knife to cut the roots apart. This is best done in the spring when the plant is still dormant, although you can divide in late autumn as well. After digging up the herb, take it to a firm table or bench to do any cutting. Then replant the divided sections and firm in well.

Chives can be divided in late winter just as the green spears start to show above ground. Dig up the clumps and gently prise the bulbets apart, replanting only five or six together and spacing about 10-15cm/4-6 in apart. This way you can create a border with only a few clumps. Mint can be dug up in the spring and divided into roots of only 15cm/6 in each. Discard and destroy all unwanted roots and firm those roots you are keeping into the soil, either in new beds or pots.

Above: A good example of well-divided chives showing strong stems and, in this case, well-formed, attractive flowerheads, which the bees will take good advantage of. **Below:** Chives can be propagated by prising them apart in the early spring and placing the bulblets in smaller clumps to produce stronger growth.

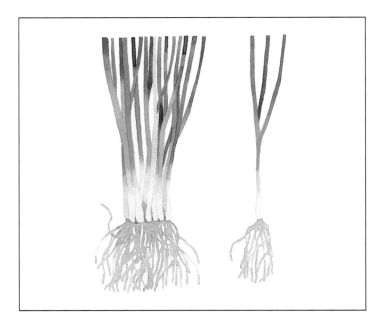

Other perennials can be divided with a fork or pulled apart. Lady's mantle and marjoram are good examples with which you can use this method. Woodruff and creeping thymes sometimes divide best in late summer while tarragon, meadowsweet and valerian can happily be divided in the early autumn.

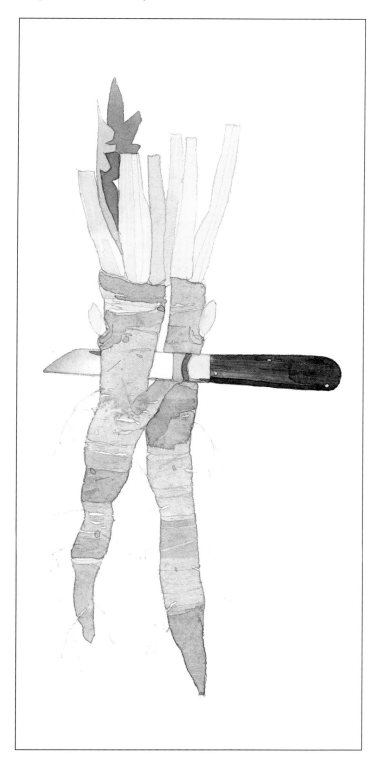

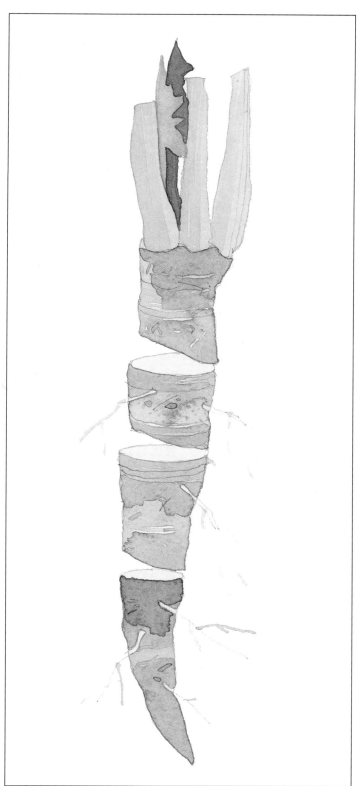

Above: Root division of lovage can be done by use of a sharp knife, without having to be too careful about the cutting. Do, however, be careful about the direction in which you make the cut, as accidents often occur when hacking through a strong root. Other herbs suitable for propagating by root division include comfrey.

Above: A lovage or comfrey root will readily produce new growth from all parts of the root.

Softwood cuttings

You can use the same compost for cuttings that you used for seeds, and plug trays make excellent containers for easy cultivation. Softwood cuttings, as the name implies, are soft top shoots of shrubby, mostly aromatic herbs and are best taken in late spring and early summer. Typical plants are: santolina, curry plant, lavender, sage, rosemary and the artemisias.

Take the tip of a vigorous shoot with no flowers and cut it off about 10cm/4in from the top. Reduce this by half and remove the lower leaves. Dip the base in hormone rooting compound (although I find this is not particularly necessary with soft herbs) and firm into the compost. For rosemary and lavender add a little more sharp sand to the mix, as it helps it to root more vigorously.

Water the cuttings well and place in a shady place outdoors, in a cold greenhouse or on a shady windowsill. Some people suggest you create a moist climate for your cuttings by placing a plastic bag over your pots with small canes to keep the plastic away from the leaves. This can speed up the process, but I have always found it difficult to keep in a lasting shape and the cuttings quite often get too wet and dampen off. This may, of course, be my own ineptitude, but the success rate of more open methods seems to confirm my belief that a good idea has been allowed to develop too readily, causing great disappointment when cuttings fail. Trial and error will determine the best way for you.

Another method, which I have found is successful with rosemary, is to take quite large cuttings and press them into the ground underneath the mother plant. The natural shade and suitable soil help the shoots to root quite easily.

Semi-hardwood cuttings

Semi-hardwood cuttings are taken in late summer and hardwood in the autumn. Suitable herbs are hyssop, lemon verbena, scented geranium, rosemary, rue, wall germander and thyme. These shoots are longer than softwood cuttings and more developed. If you can re-

Left: Always cut softwood cuttings just below a leaf node. As soon as you have taken the cutting place it in a polythene bag and tie tightly. This will ensure that the cutting is as fresh as possible when you pot it up. The end of the cutting can be dipped into hormone rooting powder, although this is unnecessary with some herbs.

move the shoot taking a little of the bark with it then this is known as a 'heel', and helps to make the cutting take more easily. Use a similar compost to the soft-wood cutting compost and add a little more sharp sand to the mixture. Place cuttings in pots, singly, in a shady area and allow to root before removing to a lighter place and the planting out. All cuttings need light and air once the new shoots begin to appear.

Layering

Herbs such as rosemary and sage can be increased by layering. This encourages a natural tendency to root when the woody stems lie close to the earth. By hold-ing the stem down with a peg (old-style clothes pegs, dolly pegs, work very well), the stem puts down roots into the soil. The stem can then be cut free from the plant and transplanted with its new root. This method can also be tried with thyme, marjoram, winter savory and hyssop.

Right An example of an 'Irishman's heel' cutting using rosemary.
Below: Layering rosemary by use of a peg. The stem of the plant can be scratched on the side entering the earth, to encourage new growth.

Mounding up

I have an old sage plant that has become rather woody with leaves appearing only at the tips. By earthing the plant up until only the tips are visible I have in effect 'layered' the whole plant. As the season goes on the stems will produce the root growth and then I can take the earth away and detach the tips with their new root systems and plant them out. If your sage plant is quite old than you can propagate a large number of new plants in this way.

The greenhouse

A cold greenhouse is a boon to any herb grower. There is no need for heat as the best time to use it is in the spring, and the natural heat of the sun is enough. As the season progresses and you grow on basil and conservatory herbs you may need to shade the glass from the sun's glare. You can buy greenhouse shading or whitewash the glass.

Above: A purple sage bush in the author's garden which has been mounded up. The herb already shows evidence of healthier growth.
Opposite: A straggly sage bush showing the beneficial effect of 'mounding up'. Using this method, you can achieve several large plants from one old bush. Extra plants can always be donated to friends.

Herbs need plenty of air as well as light, so remember to open the door as well as the overhead lights to allow the air to circulate. I remember seeing the greenhouses at a herb nursery in Scotland wide open, with myrtles growing in them in the early autumn. The plants were the healthiest I had seen all year. If you are worried about cats or birds getting into the greenhouse, then put a temporary frame of wire mesh across the entrance.

Keep your greenhouse tidy and clean and be prepared to spray for pests when the weather warms up.

When planting out in the vegetable garden you can use cloches to warm the soil beforehand and then to bring the plants on quickly. But always remember the need for air.

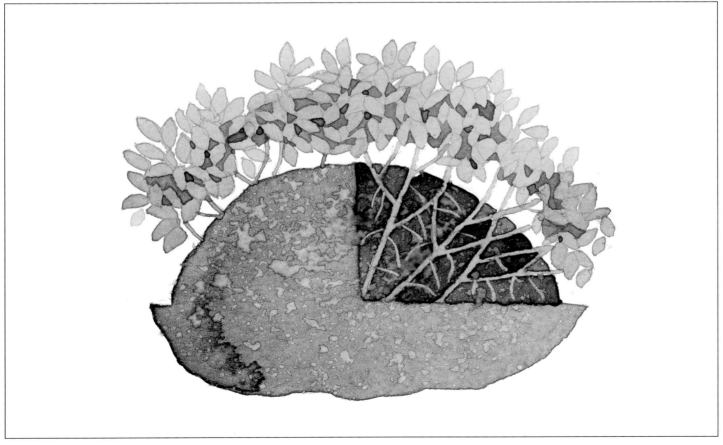

Above all do not pamper your herbs too much. I know many come from the Mediterranean, but they adapt perfectly well to temperate climates and are the stronger for having to fend a little for themselves.

Above: Lawn chamomile 'Treneague' growing on from plugs planted out on stepped beds descending to a grassy lawn. Within a few weeks these herbs will develop into a cushioned carpet. **Opposite:** A healthy gold-tipped marjoram in the spring. During the summer months it loses the variegated form, reverting to a plain green leaf, but the gold tips return the following year.

Herbs for balconies

Do not despair if you only have a balcony on which to grow herbs. You can create a little haven with your very own micro-climate by careful sheltering from the wind and packing the place with pots and containers. Many balconies are deliberately south-facing, and even a west-facing one will do. East-facing is a little tricky and north should be avoided except for growing buxus in large pots.

Given plenty of light, with warm walls and windows reflecting the heat you can have quite a jungle of herbs and flowering plants. Drainage is important, and all pots and containers should have a layer of pea shingle and broken crocks at the bottom. If you are using plastic window boxes, make sure you punch the drainage holes out at the base.

Standing plants on duck boarding helps to spread the weight and allows for excess water to drain away without being trapped. Use separate pots for each herb and only one or two containers with three or more in each. Place them at different heights and allow for plenty of depth for the roots to seek out moisture. Hanging baskets only work if you have the time to water them. If you fix them to pulleys with a cleat on the wall you can lower them for ease of watering.

All herbs in containers need to be fed regularly during the growing season. Do not overdo it but remember compost doesn't last forever. It is a good idea to lift all your pot-grown herbs and repot in new compost each year. To improve the look add a little horticultural grit to the top of the compost. This also helps to retain moisture.

Try as you might you won't be able to grow tall herbs such as fennel and lovage in the hope of achieving the same height as in the ground. But by constantly cutting them you can grow quite bushy plants and not be disadvantaged by your false environment.

— *Maintaining the Herb Garden* —

Herbs may be easy to grow, but because of their unruly nature and ability to grow on quickly, they need a good deal of attention. There is no such thing as a low-maintenance garden where herbs are concerned. With the ever-increasing pace of people's lives, both at home and at work, many people are looking for an easy way out in the garden. We have come to expect a tidy, attractive environment that needs little more than a quick dust and hoover in order to get on with the serious business of leisure. All I can say is, if you want a low-maintenance garden then concrete the yard and stand a couple of ornaments about. Herb gardens are not an easy option. They are living, breathing, developing things with the same sort of needs and care that is extended to any other living, breathing, developing creature.

Herbs need cosseting in their infancy, feeding regularly until old enough to leave home, and a safe, secure, healthy environment in which to grow and prosper. The early stages of your plants' existence have already been discussed. Once you have planted them out in your garden, then comes the task of keeping them healthy and administering to their needs. Certain woody-stemmed plants need little more than a light prune each spring. Others, however, need harvesting on a regular basis.

All herbs are 'useful' plants and need to be used. A large number, admittedly, have a built-in immune sys-

tem and seem to avoid being infected by aphid or caterpillar. Other, softer herbs such as fennel require constant vigilance. Very often the first sign of ants climbing the stalks of plants such as angelica indicates the presence of aphids, insect pests which ants 'farm' for their milk.

Pruning, clipping, feeding, mulching and pest control apply to herbs just as much as other plants. A simple regime from season to season with regular use and tender loving care can keep your herb garden looking fresh and healthy, and give the appearance of being natural and maintenance free. Taming herbs is always rewarding.

Year-round maintenance

By using the information below as a guide to the seasonal care of your herbs you can minimise problems and make the most effective use of your time.

SPRING
Spring is the busiest time of the herb year. I prefer to do all hard pruning after the worst of the frosts are

Left: A splendid topiaried cupressus 'Goldcrest' is surrounded by bold terracotta flowerpots planted with angelica. **Above:** Once the angelica had flowered the herbs were cut back and trimmed, which markedly improved the appearance of the herb bed. **Opposite:** While this is a good example of a well maintained herb garden, the flowers of sorrel (on the right) will need to be cut off to ensure good leaf growth.

over. Tall growth on hyssop, germander, marjorams, santolina, southernwood and so on have protected them from the worst effects of snow and ice. Now you need to encourage the new growth coming from the base of the plant, and the lower stems. Some herbs, such as lavender, should only be cut back to last year's new growth. Avoid cutting back into old wood. However, the artemisias in particular, as well as rue, need a hard prune – only a few centimetres above the soil – to promote new strong shoots. For a few weeks they will look bare and forlorn. No one likes to look at bare brown stems, but this is necessary if you are going to enjoy full, well-shaped bushes in the summer.

Using a sharp pair of secateurs, cut back old growth and dead flowering stems left over from the autumn. This now gives you the chance to fork over the soil

Above: In spring, all evergreen perennials can be trimmed and cut into shape. The buxus hedges have suffered a little from a late frost, but will quickly recover. **Opposite:** By late summer the chives have long since lost their flowerheads, and others, such as santolina 'Lemon Queen', rose 'Alberic Barbier' and hyssop, show the benefit of good pruning.

around the shrubby herbs and add a little bone meal or well-rotted compost. Remember not to overdo it: too much feeding can be just as bad as too little. Herbs need some food, but not an orgy of muck. Save that for the roses.

The benefit of growing old fashioned rose varieties such as the Apothecary Rose is they need very little pruning. Take off any fruit left over from last year and just clip the tips to shape the bush. Lightly fork all around and give the bushes a feed with well-rotted manure or specialist rose feed. Old fashioned roses are

Above: *Rosa gallica officinalis*, also known as the 'Apothecary Rose', 'Red Rose of Lancaster' and 'Old Red Damask', is one of the oldest roses in cultivation. During the month of June it displays beautiful, delicate flowers that crumble at the slightest touch. It is at this stage that they are ripe for harvesting for pot pourri or medicinal tinctures.

quite delicate and need careful handling – their thorns are the sharpest you are likely to encounter.

Sage plants look worse than any other herb after the winter. Do not be disheartened by this. Wait until late spring and then cut hard back to the new growth which appears from the bottom of the woody stems. To encourage these you can cut the tips off in mid-spring and propagate cuttings from them.

This is an exciting time of year for really keen gardeners who are watching for new shoots to emerge, and seeing which plants have self-seeded. It is a also a good time to observe patiently the rates of growth and the time it takes for some plants, such as evening primrose, to appear. Do, therefore, take care not to tread the soil too much, as you could be destroying newly germinated seeds. There are some herbs, including feverfew, that self-seed far too readily and can take over if allowed to do so. Be bold and remove anything you don't want. I know it seems wicked to throw away any plant, but sometimes it is necessary to be ruthless. I have seen a number of jungles, which are the result of sentimental gardeners.

Early spring is an ideal time to divide chives and lift mint for replanting. Chives can be lifted at the first sign of their reappearance and split up for stronger growth in the summer. Mint needs to be lifted in order to check its invasiveness, but also because it is a traveller and therefore is prone to die off at its original planting place. Dig up the roots that have developed over the winter and cut the new, strong roots (which have tiny fibrous root hairs showing) into short lengths. Return these to the soil with a little compost and just press them into the surface. Space each one a little distance apart and water in.

Once you have done all the spring cleaning and trimming keep an eye on the weather. In a very dry spring, you must give a light sprinkling of water to encourage the growing process. If there is reasonable moisture, then apply a light foliar or root feed.

Container-grown plants need a great deal of attention at this time of year. That thyme plant, for instance, that did very well in its small pot last year now needs to be grown on in a larger pot. All container-grown herbs can quickly become 'pot-bound'. A new lease of life in fresh compost and with room for the roots to spread can work wonders for an ailing plant, tired after the winter and in need of nourishment.

All window boxes should be replanted and large container plants such as bay and box will need a liquid feed from now on as well as regular watering. Check for any first signs of aphid and spray with a good soap-based pesticide.

SUMMER

Dead-head all roses as they die off to encourage new buds to flower. This is the season of salads, and your herb garden will be looking its best between early summer and the onset of autumn. Keep cutting back all vigorous growing herbs such as sorrel, lovage, mint, fennels, and lemon balm and use chives, parsley, basil, dill, rocket and so on.

Now is also the time to begin to harvest your herbs for drying. The simple rule that applies to harvesting any herb is, only harvest on a dry day, and even then wait until the dew has dried on its leaves and just before the sun starts to warm it enough to denude it of essential oils. The most potent time for herbs is just before they come into flower.

Most of the Labiatea family and the artemisias produce oil from tiny glands in the leaves. By waiting until the plant is just about to flower you can catch it at its best.

Late summer sees seed heads appearing and these will need to be harvested for next year's seeds and for the kitchen.(See 'Drying and Storing'.)

Continue to feed window boxes every week, and water hanging baskets daily. If the weather is very hot and dry you may need to water well twice a day

Weeding is a chore, but a necessary one, as grasses can quickly grow up through your herbs and become entangled in the roots, making it very difficult to remove them the following year. Young thyme seedlings may appear at any time from late spring through summer, and can usefully be potted on to fill any gaps evident in the autumn.

From early summer you can trim and prune bay and box plants. Topiary can be shaped and fed with a good foliar feed, hedges kept in trim and flower heads cut off if you wish to keep the tight shape. Later into the summer a mulch can be beneficial for all woody-stemmed herbs as they retain moisture and are prepared for the cold autumn nights.

AUTUMN

Autumn is the time to harvest roots. These include angelica, elecampane, marshmallow, horseradish, chicory and comfrey. Comfrey can also be divided, although I prefer to do this in the spring. Flowerheads need to be cut off as they die, and you should cut back lemon balm and evening primrose. Lavender spikes should be cut off, but do not be tempted to prune lavender until the following year. Continue to mulch and take up half-hardy perennials such as lemon verbena, scented geraniums, myrtle (if outdoors), pineapple sage, tricolor sage and basil. You will need to pot them up so they are ready to bring into the house or greenhouse where they will be protected from frosts.

If you haven't already done so in late summer, take cuttings from the scented geraniums and trim back pineapple sage and lemon verbena.

Now is the time to stop feeding and allow your herbs to rest in otder to prepare for the dormant period of winter. Early autumn is a particularly busy time for those who pickle and make jams and jellies, chutneys and vinegars, all of which will benefit from the addition of herbs in some way.

WINTER

Apart from the woody-stemmed, shrub-like herbs such as rosemary, thyme, marjoram, winter savory, hyssop and so on, many herbs die down in the winter and disappear completely until the following spring. The woody herbs need protection from severe weather with a dressing of leaf mould or well-composted forest bark. However, remember that these mulches should not be left around the plants for too long the following spring, as otherwise they will trap too much moisture around the herbs.

It is a good idea to mark where French tarragon, chives and mint are growing, so that you are not too

Petunias have been carefully placed in their pots at the base of a bay tree, helping to brighten up the bare lower stem. The strong summer leaf growth of the bay can be trimmed into shape now.

alarmed by the gaps they will leave during the long winter months.

In exposed areas it is essential to protect herbs from cold winds. Screening and spun coverings help, if they are put over the plants in extremely cold weather. Bay, unless it is near the warmth of the house, will need to be brought inside, although I have found bay trees in this country to be remarkable resilient, recovering their leaf if given the chance and responding to clipping again the following summer.

You are bound to experience some losses, sometimes, as a result of very damp winters. Treat this philosophically and enjoy the fruits of your summer labours with dried herbs and pot-pourri around the winter fires.

The evidence of late frost damage is clear on these buxus hedges. If you live in an area that is prone to late frost, then it is advisable to trim your hedges into rounded shapes during the summer, thereby avoiding the possibility of excess water settling on them.

Pruning and clipping

The grazing habits of the wild Mediterranean goats give rise to my theory that if you clip herbs lightly as if you were a wild animal foraging, then the plants recover and flourish. A fanciful theory maybe, but there is no doubt that judicial clipping and pruning is particularly beneficial to woody stemmed plants such as thyme, wall germander, box and marjoram.

Early pruning is essential to establish new growth and to create the right shape. Southernwood, wormwood, rue and sage all need to be cut hard back in the spring, hyssop a little later and lavender last of all. Some people prefer to clip lavender in the autumn, but I prefer to let it overwinter before lightly shaping it.

Most plants have an optimum height and object to being kept too low. It is as well to check what this is if

you want a dwarf variety, so you don't end up buying lavenders that spread up to a metre wide and you can't understand why they don't respond to hard cutting back. Rosemary can be harvested in moderation for most of the year, but it will take to quite hard pruning in early summer, as will bay trees.

Herb hedges

By cutting herbs into hedge shapes you stop them from flowering. In the case of rosemary and lavender I think this a shame, but I have to admit that the sight of buxus and cotton lavender with no flowers, clipped and shaped in the garden at Ham House, just outside London, is very pleasing on the eye. On a small scale though, I feel you do need cotton lavender flowers.

Hedges can be straight edged, for example with cotton lavender, obelisk or barrel shaped, which suits wall germander, or round, which is appropriate for curry plants. Buxus can be pruned from early summer onwards and produces very tight growth, making it an ideal subject for topiary.

Mulching and feeding

Mulching is a way of enriching and insulating the soil around your herb plants. Although herbs can suffer from too much moisture in areas where the soil dries out very quickly it helps, in the height of summer, to retain some water and protect the roots from burning.

Mulch can be well-rotted leaf-mould, forest bark or peat. Herbs respond best to the organic leaf-mould mulch, which can be applied lightly at first and then built up into the winter months. I like to place the leaves of comfrey about the soil and allow the natural decomposition and the work of earthworms to incorporate it into the beds. Both comfrey and yarrow are good compost activators.

Do not use a mulch on compacted clay soils. In any case, you should have dug in plenty of grit, sharp sand and well-rotted manure well before planting, and an addition of part or all of these materials can help each season. Lawn clippings are often used but should be left for a week or two and turned regularly, otherwise they are too 'hot' and also have a tendency to mat together. In the spring you need to remove as much mulch as possible to allow light and air to all of the plant, and to avoid it becoming too wet.

With the soil enriched, you can start feeding once winter has passed; feed with soluble feeds about every two weeks, gradually increasing the amount into the growing season.

If you have prepared your soil well, then you will find you need little feed, and, as I always advocate, you will not pamper your herbs too much. Although parsley, basil and some salad herbs green up well with feeding, you do not want your herbs growing too fast and becoming soft and leggy.

Pest control

Long before the introduction of chemical pesticides, people discovered the use of aromatic and bitter herbs to repel insects and vermin. In Morocco they would surround their orchards with hedges of rosemary. If you are troubled by ants then pennyroyal will deter them. I have sprinkled the leaves of pennyroyal along a windowsill, where ants were coming into the kitchen, and it was extremely effective, driving them all away immediately.

There are a number of pest repellent herbs. Traditional ones are tansy, feverfew, fleabane and elecampane. The strong odour of garlic and other alliums repel carrot fly and offer protection to roses. A number of aromatic herbs ,such as rosemary, thyme, winter savory, hyssop and marjoram, deter cabbage moth and other beetles. Mint is another herb to protect the cabbage family and deter flea beetle. Brought into the home it helps to keep flies out of the house. Rue and wormwood are the strongest smelling and most pungent of all the insect repellents.

All of these can be made into infusions with which to spray your plants. Instead of throwing the used herbs away you can spread them about among the plants as a light mulch. Soap flakes can be added to the mixture to help kill aphids, trapping them and suffocating them. Fresh herbs can be used in measures of one handful to 600 ml/1 pint of water.

I made up a garlic spray to control insect pests some years ago. I crushed 20 cloves of garlic and added a little paraffin oil. Making a pure soap solution in 300ml/½ pint of hot water, I poured this over the garlic and left it for a day before warming it up again and straining it. After boiling it I used a ratio of 1:100 parts with water.

Young 'Rougette', a lamb living in Provence, demonstrates the art of herb nibbling on a *Santolina viridis* hedge. This type of light pruning in the spring is very beneficial.

It seemed to be very effective. But everywhere stank of garlic, and when the sun caused the cork to eject like a bullet in the shed one day, it was several days before we could bear to be in there. Effective as it was I have given this one up in favour of more sweet-smelling infusions such as southernwood.

If you are plagued by insects at night in your garden, then gather a few aromatic herbs — sage, rosemary, southernwood, ru — and place them in a can or on a deep tray and ignite them with dried grass or paper. This helps to smoke them out and sweetens the air. I have used this method on a spent barbecue.

The comforting thing about all these sprays and deterrents is that they are all safe, and offer no harm to bees and other garden 'friends'. If you are lucky enough to have a toad to eat the slugs and snails, and, as we once had, a friendly neighbourhood fox that killed off the rats and mice, then you should feel very well protected.

Right: Low-growing thymes planted in gravel thrive happily in this dry environment. They will develop rapidly and will soon grow into one another. **Below:** Well-spaced culinary herbs, with mint enclosed by slates (right) and contained in a bottomless flower pot (left) can be reached by means of stepping stones.

Plant companions

In the plant world, as with the human race, there are those that get on well with each other and are beneficial, and there are those who cannot bear the sight of one another. The former, as with humans, are known as 'good companions' and these make good neighbours. Some of these – and some bad neighbours – are listed below.

Lemon balm Beneficial to other plants. Attracts bees.

Basil Grow near tomatoes to repel insects and benefit growth. Hates rue.

Borage Another friend of tomatoes, and helps to improve crops of strawberry.

Chamomile Known as 'the plant's physician'. Beneficial to ailing and sick plants.

Chives Companion plant to roses, helps to prevent black spot.

Dill A friend to cabbages but dislikes tomatoes and carrots.

Fennel Traditional flea repellent. A loner, not a good companion.

Garlic Beneficial to roses, but dislikes beans and peas.

Hyssop Good to grow among grape vines. Not good near radish.

Marigold Good companion for tomatoes, asparagus and cucumber.

Mint Friend to cabbages and tomatoes.

Nasturtium Beneficial to fruit trees, tomatoes, radish, cabbage, broccoli, broad beans. A trap for blackfly and woolly aphids. Good for general health of plants. around it.

Pennyroyal General ant repellent and mosquito repellent.

Rosemary Friend to carrots and sage. Good protective hedge.

Rue Likes raspberries, roses, but dislikes basil.

Sage Plant with rosemary, all vines, cabbages and carrots. Does not help cucumbers.

Tansy Plant near roses, cabbages, fruit trees.

Summer and winter savoury Traditional 'bean' herb. Deters bean beetle.

Wormwood Likes radish. Keeps cats and wild animals away.

All bee-loving plants are good companions to the garden in general, as they also attract hoverflies whose larvae feed on aphids. Yarrow will increase the aromatic qualities of all medicinal and fragrant herbs. Although there has been no scientific study into companion planting, the general good health of many cottage gardens and allotments are testament to the enduring theory first expounded by Pliny in the first century AD.

Culinary Uses

This is, probably, where most of us came in. I can still remember one of the most distinctive tastes, as a child, was my mother's parsley sauce. I wasn't aware at the time that I was eating a nutritious herb; but I was aware of the complementary taste it gave to the fish dish. So today, fish, without parsley sauce, doesn't seem complete.

Herbs in your diet are, without a doubt, good for you. It didn't take civilised peoples too long to realise this. The health of a nation is vital to its survival; and what better way to introduce healthy living than by encouraging the use of natural herbs to strengthen the whole system.

It is well accepted that garlic is good for the blood and, as a result, acts as a heart tonic. Herbs supplement essential vitamins, balancing the diet by a natural selection process through the taste buds. The sheer joy of eating is in the taste. Of all the senses that come into play during eating, it is the taste that makes it a pleasurable experience. Certain herbs become synonymous with certain foods – basil with tomatoes, dill or parsley with fish, rosemary with roast lamb – and we all have our favourites. In the hands of an expert, good food can be elevated into something sensational through the clever use of herbs. Herbs are, as the emperor Charlemagne suggested, 'the praise of cooks'.

However, when using herbs for cooling it is important to remember that overkill can often ruin your food. There is no need to lavish great amounts of herbs into your dishes in the misguided belief that because they are complementary, large amounts are more beneficial. As in most other things, with the use of herbs moderation is the key to success. A dish can be ruined by the addition of a whole handful of herbs, where two leaves would have been perfect.

The recipes included here are all tried and tested by myself and some very good friends, including one or two expert cooks. While enjoying them I hope that, like me, you will realise how lucky we are to be spoilt by nature's bounty.

Below: Alpine strawberry flowers appear in early summer and are quickly followed by tiny, flavourful fruit. **Right:** Angelica is a large ornamental herb with both culinary and medicinal uses.

SOUPS

Garlic or Onion Potage

From Thomas Tryon's *The Good Housewife* (1692)

Take water and oatmeal, stir it together and when it is ready to boyle bruise as much garlick or onion as you please, to make it either strong or weak, put this bruised garlick into your boyling hot gruel and brew it to and fro with your ladle that it may not boyl, for five or six minutes; then take it off and let it stand a little, then add butter, salt and bread and eat it as warm as your blood. 'Tis a brave, warm, cleansing Gruel, nothing so strong and nauseous as that which is boyled for this way you do extract the finer and purer parts of the garlic, and leaves the strong nauseous qualities behind, but on the contrary much boyling, or boyling according to custom, does destroy the good cleansing vertues and awakens the Evil.

★ ★ ★

Soupe de Sante, for Fish Days

From *The Receipt Book of Joseph Cooper,* 1654.
Cooper was cook to Charles I

Take Celery, Endive, Sorrel, a little Chervil and cabbage-lettuce well picked and washed, mince them down with a knife, squeeze the water from them, put them into a saucepan. Toss them up in Butter with a little Onion, take off all the fat, then put to them a little water from boiled Peas, and let them boil till they are tender; then put in half-a-spoonful of flour and keep moving it till it is brown. Then put in some good Fish-broth and a glass of wine, season it with Salt, pepper, an onion stuck with cloves, shred Parsley and a faggot of savoury Herbs, lay in the middle of your Soop-dish a French Roll fried having taken the crumb out at the bottom, cover the bottom of your dish with the crust of French Rolls, set it over a chafing dish of coals, lay the herbs upon them and then pour the soop upon your crusts and herbs, let it stand a while to simmer, and soak the Bread. Garnish it with Turnips and Carrots and serve it up hot.

★ ★ ★

Sorrel and Lettuce Soup with Chervil
Serves 4
1 or 2 handfuls fresh, young sorrel leaves
1 head of lettuce
50 g/2 oz streaky bacon
½ tbsp chervil
900 ml/1 ½ pints/3 ¾ cups good chicken stock (not from a cube)
salt and freshly-ground black papper, to taste

Sorrel and Lettuce Soup with Chervil

METHOD

1 Wash the sorrel and cut into fine strips. Wash and shred the lettuce.

2 Cook the bacon very gently until the fat melts; then remove the bacon pieces.

3 Cook the sorrel, lettuce and chervil (leave some for garnishing) in the remaining bacon fat until wilted. Add chicken stock and simmer gently.

4 Add seasoning to taste and garnish with the extra chervil.

★ ★ ★

Minted Pea Soup
Serves 4

2 x 400 g/14 oz tins of petit pois
200 ml/1 pint/ 2 ½ cups chicken or vegetable stock
3 handfuls of chopped mint
1 tsp castor sugar
salt and freshly-ground black pepper to taste
single cream and chopped mint, to garnish

METHOD

1 Liquidise the peas in a blender or food processor. Pour into a saucepan and add the stock, sugar, mint and seasoning. Use less stock if a thick soup is preferred.

2 Simmer for 8-10 minutes. Pour into warmed soup bowls, swirl a little cream into each bowl and sprinkle with chopped mint.

This soup can also be served chilled.

★ ★ ★

SALADS

Summer Salad of Herbs and Leaves
Serves 6-8

1 lollo rosso or salad bowl lettuce
1 handful broad-leaf sorrel (pick only fresh young shoots)
1 handful buckler-leaf sorrel (pick only fresh young shoots)
1 handful salad burnet, stripped from its stalks
1 handful rocket, stripped from its stalks
a few sprigs of mint (ginger mint gives colour and piquancy), lemon balm, tarragon, good king henry, lemon or orange
thyme, chives, garlic, chervil and fennel

Summer Salad of Herbs and Leaves

METHOD

1 Line the bowl with the lettuce leaves.

2 Toss the other ingredients and pile into the centre.

3 Dress with a light vinaigrette and decorate with marigold petals and nasturtium flowers.

The best summer salads are made with home-grown lettuce.

★ ★ ★

EGGS

Salviata – Sage Omelette

6 free-range eggs (size 3)
1 level tbsp flour
2 tbsp whole milk
1 level tbsp fresh sage, chopped
1 small garlic clove, finely chopped
50 g/2 oz/½ cup parmesan cheese, freshly grated
½ tsp salt
freshly ground black pepper, to season
1½ tbsp olive oil

The simplest and best of ingredients, fresh herbs and free-range eggs, for creating an elegant omelette.

METHOD

1 Lightly beat the eggs with a fork. Mix together the flour and milk and then beat into the eggs.

2 Add the sage, garlic, parmesan (save some for garnishing), salt and pepper.

3 Heat the oil in a large non-stick frying pan and then pour in the egg mixture. Turn the heat down immediately and let the mixture cook very gently.

4 When it has nearly all set, but still shows a pool of uncooked eggs at the top, place it under a low grill until the top is set. Turn it out and serve hot, warm or cold, sprinkled with the extra parmesan.

★ ★ ★

FISH

Pink Trout Fillets with Dill and Lime

Serves 4

50 g/2 oz/4 tbsp butter
grated rind and juice of one lime
4 pink trout fillets
2 tbsp dry vermouth (optional)
black pepper, to season

GARNISH:
1 lime
a handful of fresh dill

METHOD

1 Melt the butter in a wide shallow frying pan. Add the juice of one lime. Lay the trout fillets in the pan, skin side down, and cook gently until tender. This does not take long.

2 Remove the trout fillets and place on a warm serving plate.

3 Add to the pan juices the grated lime rind, vermouth and black pepper to season.

4 Pour the juices over the trout fillets and garnish with fronds of dill and lime wedges.

Note: You may use coriander instead of dill, but I think this takes away from the delicate flavour of the trout.

A Sauce for a Roasted Rabbit used to Henry VIII

From *The Treasurie of Hidden Secrets and Commodious Conceits* by John Partridge (1586)

Take a handfull of washed Parsley, mince it small, boyle it with butter and verjuice upon a chafing dish, season it with sugar and a little pepper grosse beaten; when it is ready put in a fewe crummes of white bread amongst the other: let it boyle againe till it be thicke, then laye it in a platter, like the breadth of three fingers, laye of each side one rosted conny (rabbit) and so serve them.

Fennel is a useful culinary herb. Add the seeds to vegetables and use finely-chopped leaves in soups.

Parsley Sauce

25 g/1 oz/2 tbsp butter
30 g/1 oz/¼ cup plain flour
600 ml/1 pint/2 ½ cups milk
salt and pepper, to taste
1 handful parsley, finely chopped

METHOD
1 Melt the butter in a saucepan. Remove from heat, add the flour and stir in with a wooden spoon, until you have a roux.

2 Add all the milk and the salt and pepper to taste. Return to the heat and stir continuously until the sauce boils. Then add your finely chopped parsley and stir in.

This is a pouring sauce. For a coating sauce use 50 g/ 2 oz/4 tbsp of butter and 60 g/2 oz/½ cup of flour.

Traditional Mint Sauce

1 tsp sugar
25 g/1 oz/2-3 tbsp mint, finely chopped
30 ml/2 tbsp boiling water
vinegar, to taste

METHOD

1 Put a small teaspoon of sugar with the finely chopped mint. Add boiling water and stir in well.

2 Leave until cold. Then add vinegar, to suit your taste.

★ ★ ★

DESSERTS

Pink Grapefruit and Mint Sorbet with Gin
Serves 6

2 x 460 g/16 oz tins pink grapefruit segments
75 g/3 oz/6 tbsp granulated sugar
100 ml/4 fl oz/½ cup gin
1 handful of mint, finely chopped

METHOD

1 Empty juice from both tins into a saucepan. Add sugar and boil for 5 minutes until a syrup forms. Cool.

2 Add the grapefruit segments and gin and then liquidize. Add the finely chopped mint.

3 Put the sorbet in the deep freezer for 1 hour. Remove and stir thoroughly, then put it back into the freezer.

4 Remove from freezer and soften in the refrigerator for an hour before it is needed.

★ ★ ★

DRINKS

Balm Wine

From *The Receipt Book of Richard Briggs* (1788), cook at The Globe Tavern,
Fleet Street and the Temple Coffee House

Take twenty pounds of lump sugar and four gallons and a half of water, boil it gently for one hour, and put it into a tub to cool; take two pounds of the tops of green balm, and bruise them, put them into a barrel with a little new yeast, and when the liquor is nearly cold pour it on the balm; stir it well together and let it stand twenty four hours, stirring it often; then bung it tight, and the longer you keep it the better it will be.

Pink Grapefruit and Mint Sorbet with Gin

Birch Wine

From E Smith's *The Complete Housewife* (1736)

The season for procuring the liquors from the birch trees is the beginning of March, while the sap is rising, and before the leaves shoot out; for when the sap is come forward and the leaves appear the juice, by being long digested in the bark, grows thick and coloured, which before is thin and clear.

The method of procuring the juice is by boring holes in the body of the tree, and putting in fossets, which are commonly made of the branches of elder, the pith being taken out. You may, without hurting the tree, if large, tap it in several places, four or five at a time; and by that means save from a good many trees several gallons every day. If you have not enough in one day, the bottles in which it drops, must be cork'd close, and rosined or waxed; however, make use of it as soon as you can. Take the sap and boil it as long as any scum rises, skimming it all the time, to every gallon of liquor put four pounds of good sugar, and the thin peel of a lemon; boil it afterwards half an hour, skimming it very well; pour it into a clean tub, and when it is almost cold, set it to work with yeast spread upon a toast. Let it stand five or six days, stirring it often, then take such a cask as will hold the liquor; fire a large match dipped in brimstone and throw it into the cask, stop it close till the match is extinguished; tun your wine, and lay the bung on light till you find it has done the working; stop it close and keep it three months. Then bottle it off.

★ ★ ★

Mint Julep

A traditional American recipe

Serves 1

4 sprigs of mint
1 lump of sugar
1 tbsp water
50 ml/2 oz/¼ cup bourbon whiskey
crushed ice

METHOD
1 Muddle the mint, sugar and water in a tall glass. Fill with ice. Add bourbon but do not stir. Decorate with fresh mint sprig.

★ ★ ★

May Wine

A traditional German recipe

Pour a bottle of good German hock or riesling into a large bowl. Add thin slices of oranges and lemons, one glass of sherry, and sugar to sweeten to your taste. Take spring flowering stems of sweet woodruff, about one dozen. Leave to steep for at least one hour and serve into glasses.

146

Sometimes other scented spring flowers are floated on top with leaves of lemon balm or lemon verbena and lemon mint might be added. If preferred it may be chilled by adding ice cubes.

★ ★ ★

Elderflower Champagne

A traditional English recipe

1 lemon
6 newly opened flowers (picked dry, before noon)
2 tbsp cider vinegar
675 g/1 ½ 1bs/3 ⅜ cups granulated sugar

METHOD

1 Pare rind from the lemon and squeeze the juice, add to flower heads, vinegar and sugar in a large pan. Cover contents with water and stir to dissolve the sugar.

2 Cover and leave to steep for two days. Strain off and pour into glass bottles with screw top lids. Store on their sides for 2-3 weeks depending on the sparkle.

3 Serve cold with a slice of lemon. It is ready for immediate consumption and should not be stored longer than a month.

Note: Since a European Union ruling in Brussels, companies outside France are unable to name their products 'champagne'. This, however doesn't prevent you calling your homemade drink by the traditional title of 'Elderflower champagne'.

★ ★ ★

Elderflower Syrup

A traditional English recipe

Take a large jug and fill it with elderflower heads and cover with non-carbonated spring water. Leave overnight in a warm room. Strain off the liquid and add more flower heads. Two hours later strain again and add fresh flower heads. After a further two hours, strain and pour into a large saucepan and add 900 g/2 lbs/4 ½ cups of sugar to each 600 ml/1 pint/2 ½ cups of liquid. Warm over a gentle heat and stir until the sugar is dissolved. You may, if you wish, add the grated rind of two lemons. Allow to cool and bottle.

This is a concentrated mixture and must be diluted for a most refreshing summer drink. Carbonated water really peps it up. You could try making this recipe with lemon balm or lemon verbena.

Medicinal Uses of Herbs

The main difference between herbal medicine and conventional medicine is in cause and effect. Modern, chemically-synthesised drugs help a doctor to treat ailments quickly by dealing with the effect rather than seeking the cause. A medical herbalist will treat a patient holistically, concentrating on the cause of the ailment and treating it accordingly.

Modern science and technology has made us believe that we can no longer help ourselves effectively. In many cases we have become lazy, relying on the expertise of professionals. Plant remedies have been gradually lost to us and, worse still, ridiculed as 'quack' remedies and 'country magic'. However, no one with any common sense is going to suggest that plants can heal in every case. Areas of modern medicine, for example in the field of heart surgery and replacement surgery, could not hope to rely on the healing virtues of herbs. But in helping to promote a healthy lifestyle and general well-being, herbs have their place in the home. And in the treatment connected with balancing the body and encouraging the healing process from within that body, qualified medical herbalists have every right to take their place next to modern medical scientists anywhere.

Considering the thousands of years of research and practice in plant medicine it seems incredible that so much is still being discovered. It is fascinating that only now can we fully appreciate the complexity of plants, and so appreciate the good and bad effects they can have on our bodies.

For example, scientists in Scotland are now conducting research on the effect that thyme has on the ageing process, while evening primrose and feverfew are just two other herbs that have recently been the subject of lengthy scientific papers. The benefits of such research on nutrition and general health are available to us because of the efforts of these scientists and technicians.

Many doctors are keen to point to the placebo effect whenever someone claims to have been helped by plant medicine. The Latin meaning of 'placebo' – 'I shall be acceptable or pleasing' – suggests an improvement in the patient's condition brought about solely by a belief that the treatment will work. But this theory also applies to orthodox medical treatments. Further, in

Above and opposite: Feverfew, *Tanacetum parthenium*, is commonly known as a 'migraine' herb, offering relief to sufferers from the debilitating headaches. The double-flowering variety (shown above) has the same medicinal properties, but care should be taken to use only one leaf, which should be wrapped in a pellet of bread in order to avoid the possibility of mouth ulcers.

controlled research on cattle, who after all have no intelligent reasoning, the effect of homeopathic treatment in the treatment of mastitis was proven beyond doubt by administering minute drops of plant drug in drinking water.

Since medieval times the phrase 'everything in moderation' has applied to the use of herbal medicine as well as other areas of our lifes. Another phrase, more in current use today, is 'less is more'. Because of the holistic nature of plant medicine, where the whole plant is used rather than an isolated constituent, then the natural balance of that plant comes into play. By increasing the amount of plant material, you do no more good than you would by increasing a dose of pills. In fact, if you take the latter course, you could upset the balance of your body and in the end, cause more harm than good.

It cannot be stressed enough that in the plant world, as in the animal world, there is bad as well as good. Always consult a good book or, better still, a qualified herbal or medical practitioner before embarking on a lengthy course of treatment.

For home first aid and for minor ailments I have included some notes and recipes for making a few herbal products at home, all of which are perfectly safe to use. But if you are in any doubt or suffer from any allergic reactions, do not go any further than reading about it.

The development of herbal medicine

Evidence that early humans had an instinct about which plants could act as medicines came with the discovery of a Neanderthal burial site in Shanidar, Iraq. Pollen from wild flowers had been placed around the body indicating the belief that these would be of use to the deceased on their journey to the next world

A similar belief by the ancient Egyptians that provision should be made for the after life has allowed us more than just a glimpse into the art of the evolving medical herbalism . Plant remedies written on papyrus in Egypt and on oracle bones in China during the Yin dynasty (*circa* 1500 BC) show a flourishing business in plant medicine. In ancient Greece, Hippocrates estab-

Interior of an alchemist's study, a painting by Eugene Isaley (1803-1886). The alchemist's practice, carried out in the Middle Ages, included a search for a universal cure to all disease, and combined the philosophical arts with science. The division between body and mind, which is so prevalent in modern scientific thinking, did not exist.

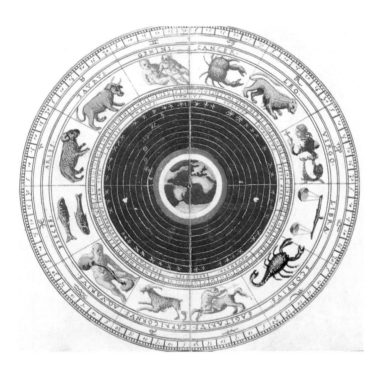

Above: Astrological charts would have assisted herbalists such as Culpeper, who aligned their herbal remedies to the influence of the stars. This 16th-century example is the Portolan Map, from the library at Lambeth Palace, London, England. **Opposite:** The foxglove, *Digitalis purpurea*, should only be used under strict medical supervision.

lished a scientific school of study into herbal medicine, expounding the theory that healing came from within the individual, assisted by diet, massage and herb remedies restoring the balance of the system. This was the first reference to holistic medicine. The Romans continued the study further, but superstition and religious belief infiltrated medicinal recipes.

While Europe experienced what has come to be known – some would say erroneously – as the Dark Ages (*circa* AD 476-1000) the Arab nations introduced the science of the pharmacy, and produced highly-educated physicians trained by Avicenna, a Persian physician who turned the study of plant medicine into a science as well as an art. Proof of his genius is witnessed in the 'Unani Tibb' system of medical practice in India today, taken from his teachings. With the rise of the monastic tradition in Europe, the study of Latin, Greek and Islamic texts gave rise to the practice and teaching of herbal medicine in all towns in which there were monasteries. By the time of Henry VIII (reigned 1485-1509), when, with the dissolution of the monasteries, the country was in danger of losing this tradition to only a handful of doctors, permission was granted by Royal Charter for all people to practise herbal medicine. So began the Golden Age of the Herbalists.

Scotland, and schools of herbal medicine, are all contributing to the furtherance of our knowledge and protection of a natural heritage which otherwise could so easily be lost.

Understanding medicinal herbs

In order to use herbs in a responsible way you first need to build up an understanding of them. In botanical studies it is essential to draw the plant. Even if you have no drawing skills, at least by attempting to draw your chosen herbs you will look that bit more closely at their structure.

First impressions are always important in life, and so with herbs; observe the growing habits, and note where the plant grows well. What type of flowers does it have? What is the structure of the leaf like? Does it grow in full sunlight or shade?

With the invention of the printing press, the herbals of Gerard, Turner, Parkinson and Culpeper reached a wide market, and the use of herbal medicine flourished during years of plague and disease, ailments which were mostly exacerbated by overcrowded unsanitary cities. But in the late 17th century the discovery of New Science began to change things dramatically.

Herbs such as Peruvian bark and sarsaparilla arrived from the New World, enabling doctors to treat specific ailments such as malaria and syphilis. Treatment of the whole body was abandoned in favour of treatment for the disease. By the middle of the 19th century orthodox medicine was overtaking herbal medicine, and when a breakthrough in the creation of synthesised drugs occurred at the end of the century, scientists could isolate components of plants and manufacture drugs such as aspirin.

After the First World War there was a serious shortage of drugs, and people were encouraged once more to use herbal medicine for treating minor ailments. An upsurge in interest coupled with a wave of nostalgia for a more natural way of life led to the prominence of women such as Maude Grieve and Hilda Leyel educating an eager public in the virtues of plants.

As a result of the work of the National Institute of Medical Herbalists (established in 1864), the Herb Society (set up by Hilda Leyel) and the emergence of properly qualified Medical Herbalists, the science of herbal medicine has not been lost to us.

There is however, still a long way to go to an official recognition of herbal practitioners and sensible licensing of herb drugs. But Research Institutes, The Chelsea Physic Garden, Auchincruivre in Ayrshire,

Above left: Clary sage, growing here with feverfew and self-heal, is used in both herbal medicine and aromatherapy. Traditionally, it was used to clear the eyes, giving rise to its name of 'clear-eye', from the Latin *sclerea*, meaning clear. **Below:** Representations of medical plants from a treatise on herbs and medicine compiled in England *c*. AD 1200.

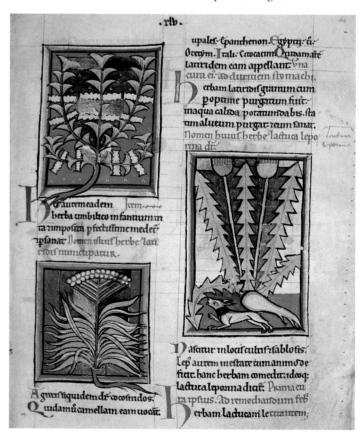

Now examine the texture, followed by the smell and then the taste. After these question have been answered, ask yourself how you personally react to the herb. Do you like it? Would you like it in your garden? What does it do for you?

Having done all this you may wish to go to your library and carry out some research. See if your impressions tally with those descriptions in the books. Check out the medicinal virtues of the herb you are studying, and see if any apply to you personally. Read up other uses and customs associated with the plant and draw some personal conclusions about the plant. Then make a tea from the leaf and flower and determine what it seems to be doing for you.

Before making a tea from a herb you must, of course, check it out carefully in your books. If you are in any doubt, then don't make it.

Herbs for the first-aid cupboard

Herb oils and lotions can be made quite easily at home using quite a small selection of herbs from the garden. Tisanes can be made from fresh herbs or from dried, and kept in airtight jars away from sunlight. Tinctures are best bought from a good apothecary shop or herbalist. Listed on page 154 are just a few essential herbs for minor ailments. If symptoms persist, and in chronic cases, always consult a medical practitioner.

Below: A selection of herbs and roots used in the preparation of home medicines. They include lavender, lemon balm, sage, comfrey root, marigold and comfrey ointments, dried chamomile flowers, variegated lemon balm, peppermint, St John's wort oil, rosemary, aloe vera and golden feverfew.

Herbs for first aid

ALOE VERA This healing succulent should be grown indoors. The juice from the fleshy leaves, when applied to burns, and, in particular, sunburn, will offer immediate relief.

CHAMOMILE A calming sedative tea and syrup. Good for fractious children.

COMFREY Made into an ointment or compress for all bruises and swellings.

FEVERFEW One leaf rolled in a pellet of bread for migraine sufferers. Also used as a tisane for depression.

LAVENDER Lavender oil for minor burns and scalds. Also to relieve discomfort from insect stings. Mixed with rosemary and basil for tired limbs and muscle strain.

LEMON BALM A tea for indigestion and colds.

MARIGOLD (CALENDULA) Antiseptic cream for minor cuts. Can also use a fresh infusion of flowers. Diluted tincture for cold sores.

PEPPERMINT Good tea for colds when mixed with yarrow and elderflower. Also for colic and flatulence. Aids the digestion.

ROSEMARY Useful for headaches; mix with lavender and basil for a good massage balm.

PURPLE SAGE For sore throats, sore gums, tightness in the chest region. A traditional 'grief' herb.

ST JOHN'S WORT Made into an oil for cuts and bleeding. Also useful for burns and scalds.

One extra tincture I would add to any herbal first aid cupboard is Bach's Rescue Remedy, which can be bought from chemists and herbalists. This tincture is invaluable for treating any kind of shock. I also use it to calm my cats on Guy Fawkes night, and for myself if I am driving on a long journey by motorway. Just four drops in a glass of water, or orange juice, is enough to calm the whole system – safely.

There are almost certainly other herbs you may like to include in your first-aid collection. Within a medicinal bed I would certainly include, for myself, nettle, parsley, yarrow and, if possible, use the shade of an elderflower tree for herbs such as mint and comfrey. Garlic as an all-round preventative and blood tonic might also be included.

Herbal preparations

There are many ways to make up herbal preparations, depending on your needs. The most common are: infusions, infused oils and creams and ointments. Others are: poultices and compresses, tinctures, vinegars and smoking mixtures.

INFUSIONS AND TISANES This is the most common form of medicinal treatment. It can be taken as a tea, or as a gargle, applied to the affected area as a douche or lotion, added to a bath or used as for inhalation or fumigation. The method is quite simple. Simply pour 600 ml/1 pint of boiling water over 25 g/1 oz of dried herbs in a teapot and allow to infuse for up to 10 minutes. Then strain and drink. You can add honey to sweeten the tea. If you are using fresh herbs you will need to add more as they retain water. Always collect herbs in the early morning before the sun begins to warm them, and after the dew on them has dried.

For inhalations just pour boiling water over 5-10 ml/1-2 tsp of the herb in a bowl and place a towel over your head, breathing in the steam through your nose and breathing out through the mouth.

When using herb roots you will need to make a decoction. Again, use 600 ml/ 1 pint of water to 25 g / 1 oz of herbs. Place in a saucepan with a light lid and simmer for about 10-15 minutes. After straining off the liquid, return it to the pan and removing the lid, reduce to one third. This can then be turned into a syrup or kept in the fridge for three or four days.

SYRUPS Make a tisane, then slowly dissolve 12 oz of sugar to a syrup. Pour into clean bottles, well labelled.

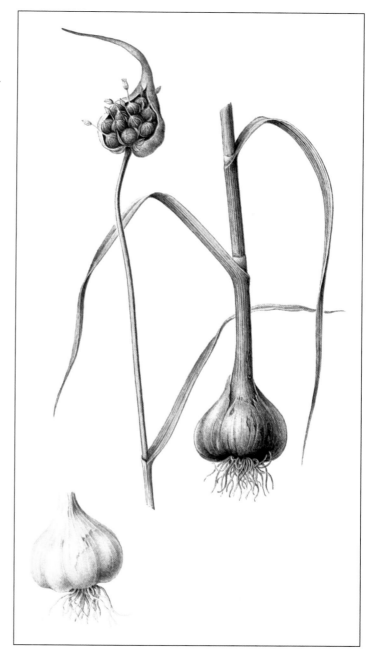

Garlic is one of nature's great promoters of good health, as well as a wonderful flavouring for food. Taken in moderation it helps to tone up your digestive system, and although it smells strong on the breath, you can sweeten the breath after eating by chewing a leaf of parsley.

INFUSED OILS The best method for this preparation is to use a water bath, or bain marie. Avoid using aluminium containers. If you do not have a water bath, then you can improvise by placing a small pan inside a larger one, resting the smaller pan on two spoons. Put water in the larger pan and place your herbs and oil into the inner pan. Use a tight lid.

Chop up your fresh herbs or roots and use 25 g/1oz of your chosen herb to 600 ml/1 pint of oil. Almond

Herbal Applications

INFUSIONS AND TISANES Teas for drinking or strained for compresses or added to bath water.

SYRUPS Effective for coughs and upper respiratory infections; also for children, being sweet and therefore more palatable.

INFUSED OILS Particularly good for massaging tired limbs and relieving cramps and spasms.

CREAMS AND OINTMENTS For application to cuts and abrasions; also for minor scalds and burns.

POULTICES AND COMPRESSES To stimulate the skin and aid circulation; also for speeding up the healing of wounds and elimination of bacteria

TINCTURES Tinctures are alcohol based and should be used only with professional advice.

VINEGARS As washes, gargles, rinses, disinfectants, antiseptics and to reduce some itchy skin conditions.

SMOKING MIXTURES For herb tobaccos.

Opposite: The evening primrose has become one of the most fashionable medicinal herbs in current use. To make the oil many more plants than are illustrated in this border would be needed. As a garden flower it offers late afternoon and evening interest, for this is when the flowers open, inviting the bees to an end-of-the-day forage.

oil is the best, but quite expensive. Grape seed oil is a good alternative and has the distinction of being odourless. Simmer for two hours and then strain off the oil and discard the herbs. Repeat the process with fresh herbs for another two hours.

The resulting oil is quite concentrated and is most effective as a massage oil and for putting in the bath.

CREAMS AND OINTMENTS Taking your infused oil, and, using the same bain marie, add 25 g/1oz of beeswax, stirring it in over a low heat. As soon as the mixture is well blended, pouring it immediately into sterilised jars.

To sterilise jars and bottles, simply wash well and then dry in a low oven, or use Milton sterilising solution and dry as before.

POULTICES AND COMPRESSES Both poultices and compresses stimulate the skin by the use of heat and allow the herbs to be absorbed through the skin. Poultices are made with pulped vegetables mixed with herbs and a small amount of oil. Spread the mixture while hot between a double layer of cotton gauze, then lay it on the fine grill of a sieve and steam over boiling water. Compresses are ways of applying infusions and decoctions to the affected area. After soaking a cloth in the infusion, wring it out and apply at once.

TINCTURES I would recommend buying tinctures from a chemist or herbalist. Alternatively, consult a qualified herbal practitioner.

VINEGARS Vinegars have been used both internally and externally for many years. They are easy to make, and are ready to use within one week of preparing.

Dilute water and vinegar in equal parts using cider or malt vinegar. Add a handful of herbs for every 600ml\1 pint of solution. Place in a wide necked jar with a screw-top lid and put in a dark place for at least

Herbal Recipes With Medicinal Uses

COLTSFOOT SYRUP

A good remedy for chesty coughs.

Use 25 g/1 oz coltsfoot to 600 ml/1 pint water. Place in a saucepan and cover with a tight lid. Simmer for 10-20 minutes, then strain off the liquid and discard the herbs. Reduce the liquid to one-third. Dissolve 275-350 g/10-12 ozs of brown cane sugar into the liquid, over a low heat. Allow to cool and pour into a clean bottle and label.

To preserve the syrup, you can add 1 part vodka to 3 parts syrup, but omit the vodka when giving to children. Lemon juice will reduce the sweetness.

Dose: 10 ml/2 tsp three times a day. 5 ml/1 tsp for children, and 2.5 ml/1/2 tsp for babies.

ROSEMARY, LAVENDER AND BASIL MASSAGE BALM

This massage balm can be used on tired muscles and limbs.

To 600 ml/1 pint of oil, add herbs amounting to no more than 25 g/1 oz. The ratio is 2 parts rosemary and lavender to 1 part basil. Place in a bain marie and heat gently for two hours. Remove from the heat and strain off the oil. Place fresh herbs in the oil and simmer for a further two hours. Strain and discard the herbs. Allow to cool, then bottle and label.

CALENDULA OINTMENT

Place 25 g/1 oz of marigold petals in 600 ml/1 pint of oil and make an infused oil, as with massage balm. After straining the second preparation add 25 g/1 oz of beeswax and stir gently over a low heat until the wax has blended in. Allow to cool in clean jars before sealing.

ST JOHN'S WORT OIL

Put a good handful of flowers in a wide necked jar and top up with almond or grapeseed oil. Stand the closed jar in the sun for two weeks. Strain off the red liquid and bottle.

LAVENDER RUB

This is particularly good for tired, aching feet.

Fill a jar with lavender flowers and cover with surgical spirit (available from chemists). Seal the jar and place in the sun for two weeks. Strain off the liquid and bottle.

one week. Turn occasionally. Strain off the herbs and pour into a clean bottle

SMOKING MIXTURES Smoking mixtures have been used for treating asthma and bronchial complaints. Simply mix your dried herbs with 5 ml/1 tsp of honey and 20 ml/4 tsp of water. Dry in the open for a few days and when it feels slightly damp, store the mixture in air tight containers.

Opposite: The time to harvest coltsfoot, *Tussilago farfara,* is in the early spring when the mucilaginous content of its flowerheads and young leaves is at its most powerful. When made into a syrup it relieves those late winter coughs and calms the respiratory passages, coating the tiny hairs in the airway with its soothing liquid. It is a useful herb for asthma sufferers.

Homeopathy:
Dr. Bach's Flower Remedies

In the 1920s, Dr Edward Bach, an eminent bacteriologist, took the courageous step of following his instincts and researching the healing effects of wild flowers. Probably influenced by the teachings of Samuel Hahnemann, who pioneered homeopathic medicine in the early 19th century, he began the search for the natural power of diluted substances in plants that aid the body in healing. It was Hahnemann who expounded the theory that like cures like – *Similis similibus curentur.*

In the world of herbal medicine the emphasis is on restoring the balance of the body to a 'healthy' state, both physically and mentally. It would seem that by introducing substances into the body that mirror the complaints, this triggers off a complicated system of defences that then fight and eventually overcome the condition. The process of administering the substance involves diluting it to an enormous degree, so that, incredibly, hardly a molecule of the original drug remains in the solution.

Experimental trials have shown this to be an effective form of treatment of disease, but much of it has yet to be comprehended by a cynical section of the medical profession.

It may have been a similar cynicism that drove Edward Bach to turn his back on conventional medicine and seek a universal truth for curing our ills. If the theory of psychosomatic illness leading to physical manifestation of illness is to be followed, then stress and worry need to be confronted in their early indications. Dr Bach was deeply interested in the temperament of his patients, and how it affected their personalities. This is an accepted theory of holistic medicine today.

Coupled with his love of plants and the countryside, Edward Bach developed a seemingly fanciful theory of dew being steeped in the curative essence of a plant simply by the power and warmth of the sun's rays. He took this a stage further by infusing flowers in natural spring water exposed to the sun. The result was a tincture, which was then stabilised in brandy. The cry of 'quack' could be heard all the way to the General Medical Council.

But, the proof, as we well know, is in the eating; and treatment with Bach's flower remedies was proving to be successful. His work centred on the human condition. Examples of tinctures for alleviating anxieties and other complaints, and so strengthening the immune system are: *Clematis vitalba*, for those who tend to dream; agrimony, for those who worry while hiding behind a cheerful facade; star of Bethlehem, for shock; rock rose, for terror; felwort, for those with self-doubt; aspen, for fear; and impatiens, for irritability and impatience.

There are 37 plants in all, and some are grouped together as in his famous 'Rescue Remedy'. I have used this remedy for shock, accident, fear of driving on motorways and even for fright induced by fireworks on Guy Fawkes night, in my cats. Two or three drops placed on the cat's nose, which is then quickly licked off, does the trick.

As a human remedy, you can administer the drops in water or orange juice, and they can even be applied to the wrists of people who are in a state of catatonic shock. The Rescue Remedy has the most calming effect without side effects, and it is completely safe. The ingredients are: rock rose, old man's beard, impatiens, cherry plum, and star of Bethlehem, all in a grape alcohol solution.

I am most grateful to the perseverance, courage and technical brilliance of this gentle doctor, who followed a theory to its ultimate tested limits and gave us a glimpse into the power of nature.

Today, the staff at the Dr. Edward Bach Centre in England continue their excellent work. The address is Mount Vernon, Sotwell, Wallingford, Oxfordshire, OX14 5JX.

Aspen, one of the plants on which Edward Bach based his remedies. It is useful for people who are fearful.

Teas and Tisanes

erb teas originated from the French *tisane*. A tisane is looked upon as a herbal remedy for minor complaints of the digestion, a common cold or insomnia. Tisanes are aromatic; a Frenchman sees no reason why he should take a medicine that is not palatable, so the idea of a refreshing herb tea, which has the added bonus of balancing the system as well, soon became popular in other parts of Europe, and spread from there. Meadowsweet (for acid stomachs), rosemary (to invigorate) and chamomile (to help you sleep) are favourites; and I take all of these. You can also make a blend from three herbs. Yarrow, peppermint and elderflower are a good combination for 'flu and colds. I try a mixture of St John's wort, lemon balm and chamomile for sleeplessness; and meadowsweet, chamomile and peppermint for a digestive.

Herb teas suit individual tastes and, while one may work for someone else, it may not necessarily work for you. Get to know the herbs you like and research them well before taking them. Most aromatics are quite safe, but you should never take any herbal tea for a prolonged period of time. If you are taking the tea as a medicine and symptoms do not show any sign of improving after three or four days, then stop taking the tea and try another one. Equally, if you show signs of improvement then stop taking the tea and allow your body to continue the healing process.

Above: Digestive tonics are made by infusing herbs in wine. They are frequently used in some European countries as an appetite stimulant. Herbs for tonics include thyme, marjoram, chamomile and rosemary.

If you wish you can use the tea as part of a study of chosen herbs, examining constituents, virtues, habit and so on. By infusing the herb you can experience where the warmth of the drink seems to go and what beneficial effects you feel from taking it. This will help to build up an overall picture of the herb and increase your understanding of the whole plant.

Making a herbal tea

If using dried herbs, measure out 5ml/1 teaspoon per person and place in a teapot or other covered container. If you are using fresh herbs then double these amounts. Pour boiling water over the leaves and flowers and allow to stand for 5-10 minutes. Strain off and drink. You may wish to add honey to sweeten the

Above: A peppermint tisane, preferably made from freshly-picked leaves, helps in the relief of nausea, colic and flatulence.

A tea study: Sage (*Salvia officinalis*)

Custom Put sage leaf in a book to aid memory.

Properties Aromatic (essential oil); dry (astringent); bitter (promotes saliva); heavy, musty; cool and cleansing to the mouth; warming and comforting inside; promotes sweating; stimulating, invigorating; friendly.

Uses (Book research) Antiseptic (wounds); sore throats (gargle); stimulant nerve tonic (lifts the vital spirit) - two parts sage to one part basil for nervous exhaustion; lethargy (essential oil added to bath water); digestive tonic.

Medicinal Expectorant; bronchitis; mucous asthma; fever herb, especially stuck fevers – drink cold to relieve sweating (and also works to promote and arrest sweating); dries up breast milk; good for promoting pregnancy, but, it must not be taken during pregnancy; good antiseptic for all areas below the diaphragm; helps to relieve grief, as it opens up the chest region.

This is one of nature's 'cure-alls'.

Note: Sage is rich in thujone, which, if taken in large quantities, can upset the balance of the body. Do not drink for more than two weeks at one time.

Constituents Up to 2.8 per cent volatile oil (this includes thujone, camphors, pinine, borneol, linalool etc.); oestrogen substances; salvin and carnosic acid; flavenoids; phenolic acid; condensed tannins.

taste. Do not be tempted to put more than you need in the teapot, it will make the tea too strong. By experimenting, you will find the right proportion to suit your taste. Not all teas appeal to all people. If you don't like it, don't drink it.

For heartburn, make a chamomile tea as directed above. Keep it covered in a teapot, or cover the cup while infusing. An anti-spasmodic can be made from ginger root. Boil the root for 4-5 minutes and add cinnamon to taste. This is good for stomach cramps and travel sickness.

Basil is good for nausea, as is marjoram, which is also recommended for flatulence and asthma. For headache, you can try lavender flowers or lemon balm.

Digestive tonics

Bitter herbs are used as digestive tonics. Tonics stimulate and strengthen the digestive system and the liver. In Italy it is the custom to take a half glass of bitter herbs before a meal. These carminative herbs signal to the stomach that a meal is on the way, and calm the active digestive juices.

A Recipe for a Digestive Tonic

4 sprigs of rosemary
A bunch of thyme
6 sprigs of marjoram
10 chamomile flowers
4 leaves of rue
⅓ cinnamon stick
6 cloves
Red wine

METHOD

1 Place the fresh herbs and flowers in a large, wide – necked jar. Add the piece of cinnamon stick and the cloves. Pour the red wine over to cover and fill jar.

2 Seal the jar and store in a cool dark place for two weeks, turning occasionally. Strain off the wine and then bottle.

3 To use, take ½ glass in the evening, half an hour before your meal.

Domestic Uses

The most common use of herbs in the home today is in floral decoration. In a way this is not so far removed from the days when herbs were used to sweeten the air in smoke-filled houses that also reeked of all kinds of filth. As tastes became more refined these herbs became known as strewing, or

Woodruff is a traditional strewing herb: it has been collected and cultivated in herb gardens since the Middle Ages. It imparts a sweet smell of new-mown hay, particularly when cut and allowed to dry naturally. The white flowers die off in the summer, but this is the best time to harvest the herb.

manger, herbs, suggesting their use to sweeten the straw in the baby Jesus' manger.

Traditional strewing herbs are woodruff, meadowsweet, thyme, pennyroyal, lavender, roses, violets and winter savory. Of all these I love to bring woodruff into the house in the summer. Tied in bunches to hang in the kitchen it appears to have no scent at all, until it dries. Then with each passing day it gives off a heady smell of new-mown hay and reminds you of the country every time you walk past it.

Lavender has a very refreshing scent. After drying, place it in open bowls so that you can dip your fingers in it as you pass by. It sweetens the air and lightens your senses too. Lavender used to be burned in a sickroom to fumigate it, and at one time lavender bags were very fashionable – you can still find them in some craft shops to this day. But there is no reason why you should confine yourself to lavender in bags, sachets or small drawstring bags. A mixture of sweet-smelling wild flowers or various dried herbs can be used, whichever suits your nose.

The traditional nosegay was so called because it was carried close to the nose to disguise foul smells from the city drains and crowded places. A drop or two of essential oil on a tissue can have the same effect. There are some herbs that repel moth and make good fresheners at the same time. Southernwood, *Artemisia camphorata,* and camphor plant are all effective. They can either be tied up in bunches or placed in cotton bags which can then be hung as near as possible to the probable source of infestation.

Another favourite form of room freshener is pot pourri. Endless combinations can be achieved by mixing all kinds of dried petals and leaves with a fixative – such as orris root – to preserve them. I have a simple carrier basket by the fire with a selection of scented geranium leaves and old-fashioned rose petals, which has lasted all winter long. Other suitable containers include elaborate porcelain jars and pots with perforated lids which release the scent into the room. When the fragrance of the mixture begins to fade you can add a few drops of essential oil to cheer it up .

Burners, or vaporisers, for essential oils have a small dish placed above a small candle to warm the oil and allow its scent to pervade a room. If you are using pure essential oil it is best to mix it with a carrier such as grapeseed oil, or a few drops of water. The use of these burners is far preferable to aerosol sprays and there is no risk to the atmosphere. Apart from that, they do smell much better.

If you have cats, then do remember to dry some catnip and keep it in a sealed jar. Whenever you want to give them a treat, take a little of the dried herb and strew it on the carpet. They love it. You can, of course, make a small felt mouse and fill it with catnip as a toy for your pet.

Scented bookmarks can be made by drying the leaves of costmary. This was known as 'Bible leaf' because it was put to this use in monasteries. The leaf, once dried, takes on a translucent quality and retains its balm-like scent for ages. It won't stain the leaves of your book either.

Herbs can and have been used for all sorts of household uses in the laundry too. At one time when housewives had sheets to dry, they often placed them over box hedges. In this way the sheets were nicely scented for the bedroom. Today bunches of woodruff and meadowsweet can be placed between the sheets of the bed after making.

A mass of sweet woodruff happily invading this narrow border beneath a canopy of hop, which is growing up a tree trunk in the author's garden. The scent on a warm summer's evening can be intoxicating.

Above: Costmary, or alecost, is also known as 'Bible leaf'. It makes a soft-scented bookmark that dries within the pages and has the added advantage of not leaving a stain. The finely-toothed leaves should be picked when young, as in this example. **Opposite:** A simple herb wreath with which to decorate a door. The aromatic herbs will dry and so release their fragrance to welcome any visitor to the house.

The art of dyeing

The art of dyeing using plant material is not entirely lost. It has just been overtaken by chemical dyes. It is, however, necessary to use a chemical mordant of iron, alum, chrome or tin to make the dye permanent. The soft colours obtained from herbs can quickly fade without a mordant. Yellows and brown are the simplest colours to make, but plants such as madder can produce quite strong oranges which are closer to being red. Quite a lot of plant material is needed, so rather than denude your garden you can buy dried materials. Even in the earliest descriptions of the dyeing process, the need for a special building is suggested. Jean Hellot in *The Art of Dyeing* (1789) says, 'Your Dye house must be spacious and lightsome, and as near as possible to a running stream, water being absolutely necessary for preparing your Woolens and for rinsing them after they are dyed.'

Dyeing is quite a smelly process and water should be close at hand. You will also need a large dye bath, preferably stainless steel, a bucket and bowl, wooden tongs, stirrers, a measuring jug, a pair of scales and rubber gloves. You need to protect your hands from the chemicals in the mordant and to avoid dyeing yourself. Jean Hellot goes on to describe using a cold vat with urine.

Four pounds of Indigo powdered into a gallon of vinegar. Leave to digest over a slow fire for 24 hours. Pound in a mortar and add a little urine. Afterwards put in half a pound of madder mixing well with a stick. Pour into a cask containing 50 gallons of urine … It is of no consequence whether it be stale or fresh. Stir morning and evening for 8 days.

I understand that in Scotland in the 19th century as much as 3000 gallons of human urine were collected daily for the manufacture of Harris Tweed.

Herbs were used, as they are to this day, to scent soaps for the household. They can also be used to make furniture creams and polishes. In Elizabethan times it was customary to polish furniture with bunches of lemon balm. In Shakespeare's play *The Merry Wives of Windsor,* one of the characters, Anne Page says: 'The several chairs of order look you scour/With juice of balm, and every precious flower.'

The natural oils not only brought out the shine but scented the furniture as well. Horsetail is rich in silica and has been used to scour saucepans; because of this it became known as 'pewterwort'. The only unfortunate thing about horsetail is its invasive nature. It is one of the most primitive plants alive today, and dates back to prehistoric times. Horsetail is therefore is one of nature's great survivors.

Wreaths, tussie mussies and herb trophies

Herbal wreaths have been popular since the times of the Romans. Simple wreaths of bay were used then to adorn the heads of heroes and champions of war; also for poets and artists. The wreath is symbolic of the holistic nature of life and represents the continual cycle

and belief in immortality. You can make up scented wreaths that impart their scent as the herbs dry on them, or you can create a wreath to suit a wedding, or religious festival.

We usually associate wreaths with Christmas, but they can just as well be made to celebrate Easter or Advent. Artemisias make a good base, with rosemary and lavender to fill them out. I like to add cinnamon sticks and nutmegs tied with ribbons to winter wreaths. You can also place your wreath in a tray or bowl lined with moss to retain moisture and use it as a table decoration. All sorts of herbs that dry well can be used, and cones from evergreen trees as well as dried fruit added to your design.

Above: A herb trophy can contain all sorts of messages to a loved one or friend. **Opposite:** A tussie mussie is easy to make, although you can elaborate on the design of the paper holder, as shown here.

Herb pillows have long been enjoyed to aid relaxation and sleep. Hop pillows have traditionally been used as sleep pillows, but you can make up any mixture of dried herbs, rather in the same way as you would make up a pot-pourri. Placed inside a lining of muslin it can then be inserted into any pillow material, for example velvet, brocade or cotton. There is no need to make the pillow very large, the scent will remain for some weeks. Herbs to use include lemon balm, thyme, rosemary, southernwood, hops, scented geraniums, lemon verbena and lavender.

Large bouquets of herbs are known as 'trophies' and smaller posies are 'tussie mussies'. Tussie mussies originated from sweet smelling posies carried by ladies to ward off bad smells and, reputedly, infectious germs. Trophies were given as presents and could have a symbolic significance depending on the herbs included. Rosemary indicated friendship, southernwood was a love token and symbol of good luck and sweet marjoram brought joy. You can make up a saint's trophy or one made of flowers from Shakespeare. I like to plunder the garden in mid-summer and gather as many as look beautiful into a trophy for the flower vase.

Herb recipes

Recipes for polishes and pot-pourri have been handed down from one generation to another. The introduction of housekeeping manuals in the 18th century by such women as Susanna Whatman, Elizabeth Smith and Hannah Glasse led eventually to the publication of Mrs Beeton's definitive book on household management, in 1860. Here is a herb recipe for cleaning floors from Hannah Glasse's *Servant Directory* published 100 years earlier.

Take tansy, mint and balm; first sweep the room, then strow the herbs on the floor, and with a long hard brush rub them well over the boards till you have scrubbed the floor clean. When the boards are quite dry, sweep off the greens and with a dry rubbing brush, dry rub them well, and they will look like mahogany, of a fine brown, and never want other washing. This gives a sweet smell to the room ... You may use fennel or any sweet herbs that are green, or what you can get; but tansy, mint, balm and fennel are the best herbs.

A Victorian recipe for Pot-pourri comes from *Fragrant Flowers and Leaves* by Donald McDonald (1895).

Gather early in the day and when perfectly dry, a peck of Roses, pick off the petals and strew over them three quarters of a pound of common salt. Let them remain two or three days, and if fresh flowers are added, some more salt must be sprinkled over them. Mix with the roses half a pound of finely pounded bay salt, the same quantity of allspice, cloves and brown sugar, a quarter of a pound of gum benzoin, and two ounces of powdered orris root. Add one gill of brandy and any sort of fragrant flowers, such as orange and lemon flowers, lavender and lemon-scented verbena, and any other sweet-scented flowers. They should be perfectly dry when added. The mixture must be occasionally stirred and kept in close-covered jars, the covers to be raised only when the perfume is desired in the room. If after a time the mixture seems to dry, moisten with brandy only, as essences too soon lose their quality and injure their perfume.

This appears to suggest that making pot-pourri is terribly complicated and builds up the sort of mystique that

Furniture polish

Modern methods of making furniture polish and floor polishes, use beeswax, turpentine, linseed oil and soap flakes. Here is a simple recipe from an Irish friend of mine, who now lives in France. It is lovely and creamy and you can add an infusion of rosemary, lavender, or lemon balm to scent it:

Melt 1 (medium) candle and 75 g/33 oz of beeswax in a small saucepan. Add 600ml/1 pint of real turpentine. Dissolve 10ml/2 tablespoons of soap powder (flakes) in 600ml/1 pint of hot water and add to the mixture. It will look milky at this stage. Put the saucepan in a basin of cold water to cool and thicken. Put the polish into a screw-top bottle.

Above: In these two fine porcelain pot pourri baskets the sweet-scented herbs become invisible when the delightfully dainty, perforated lids with daisy motifs are placed over them. **Previous page:** Even the smallest flower arrangement can be very effective by the economical use of flowering herbs and stems. This is an excellent example of the adage that less is more.

surrounds it today. In fact, with a little imagination, enough plant and flower material, with the addition of a fixative such as orris root – which is readily available at health food shops and pharmacists – you can make it up very easily. Choose your favourite flowers and leaves, dry them well in a cool airy place and add whatever you like in the way of orange, lemon peel and so on, and just remember to keep them in clean and air tight, sealed jars.

Pouncet boxes

In Shakespeare's play *Henry IV Part 1* Harry Percy, known as 'Hotspur', describes his meeting with a limpid royal messenger, sent to the field of battle to ascertain the number of captured prisoners. Hotspur describes the 'popinjay' as 'neat and trimly dressed', and 'perfumed like a milliner'. But, the worst of all, he carries with him a pouncet box to disguise the smell of carnage. In the 16th century the fashion grew for small boxes with perforated, or pounced, lids, which were used to carry scented herbs and snuff. They were very small and made of gold, silver, wood or, in some cases, dried paste. These were very popular with ladies, and much to Hotspur's disgust, they were also popular with fops and dandies.

Pomanders

Pomanders derived their name from the French, *pomme d'ambre*, meaning an apple of ambergris. The simplest type of pomander is made from an orange stuck with cloves. To make a pomander ball, take a firm orange and press cloves into the skin, close together until the whole orange is covered. Put into a bowl with mixed spices (cinnamon, cloves, powdered ginger and grated nutmeg) and 15 ml/3 tablespoons of orris root. Turn the orange about in the mixture until you have filled in all the cracks. Leave the pomander in the bowl overnight and turn again the next day. When it has dried out you can hang it up with ribbon, threaded through with a large-eyed needle. Lemons and limes can also be used. The scent will last for weeks.

Pomanders, herbal weaths, pot pourri – all these wonderful and fragrant things come into their own in the winter months when so much of the herb garden is just a memory of warm days and sweet scents. It is comforting to think that these captured scents will return again the following year, and thereby allow the cycle of fragrance to continue.

The border in early spring shows a perfect selection of contrasting herbs grown for floral decoration. The fronds of fennel in the background are useful in providing a soft backdrop to hard stems.

Cosmetic Uses of Herbs

Homemade herbal preparations for hair, nails, eyes, skin and body present a purely natural alternative to the mass produced products so expensively packaged today. They also give you the added satisfaction of knowing that whatever you use, no animals have suffered in the preparation of your lotion, oil and so on. Of course, you will have to devote a certain amount of time and effort to make your herbal cosmetics, but many of them can be bottled or put in jars to keep. Some require infusions, which takes about as much time as making a cup of tea.

Once you begin to use them, consider the inner self as well. Diet can be a strong contributory factor in having a good clear complexion, and fingernails are a good indicator of health. Look after the inner body and the outer body is likely to be more attractive. Avoid chemically based beauty products and your skin can behave naturally. Spots are often a sign of toxins in the system. Start by attacking from within, to expel those harmful poisons in the blood stream; then the skin lotion, when applied, can work more effectively. If you consult a medical herbalist you will certainly be asked to give some idea of what you have eaten over the past week; the herbalist can then investigate your diet and adapt it accordingly to improve your outer appearance. The idea is to promote moderation – moderation in all things applies as much to eating and drinking as any other pursuit.

It is worth noting here that not all herbs react well on the skin. Some people will have allergic reactions to certain plants, and it is as well to carry out a 'patch-test' with the herb if you are in any doubt about this. Apply a small amount of lotion, or oil, to your skin and cover with a plaster (or lint with bandage if you are allergic to sticking plaster). After a suitable period of time, ideally 24 hours, check to see if your skin shows any signs of a reaction. The skin may be sore or angry looking. In the case of allergic reactions, stop using the substance immediately and, if necessary, seek professional advice as soon as possible.

You do not need any special equipment to make these preparations but it is advisable to use clean pans and utensils. A measuring jug and a set of scales are useful items; glass containers can be old, but be sure to sterilise them before use. When making ointments al-ways have the jars ready to hand so you can transfer the preparation before it begins to set. Finally, please avoid using old aluminium pots and saucepans: they can taint your cosmetics.

Herbal shampoos and conditioners

The aptly named soapwort is an ideal base for herbal shampoos. The leaves produce a natural lather and can be made into a strong infusion, then left to simmer for five minutes.

For dark hair, use a mixture of rosemary and sage in an equally strong infusion – a good handful of herbs to 250 ml/¼ pint of water. Allow to cool and add to the soapwort infusion at a ratio of three parts soapwort to one part herbal infusion. For fair hair, use chamomile and yarrow. After washing, use a herbal rinse made from a previously prepared infusion of any of the above herbs, or one made from nettle, parsley, burdock root (a decoction in this case) or southernwood.

For men's beards, the application of essential oils such as basil, sage of rosemary added to a base oil (grapeseed or olive oil) and brushed into the beard after washing helps to keep it healthy looking and helps to retain its sheen.

A tip for women with fair facial hair: apply the juice of a lemon to gently bleach it away.

Preparations for nails and hands

The condition of our nails can often be a guide to our general health, and, as with general appearance, diet is an important factor in nail care. Eat plenty of protein – fish, pulses, nuts, dairy products and fresh fruit. Brewers yeast can often supplement your diet, and

The soft colours of herbal preparation indicate the gentle quality of their restoring properties. Containers of different shapes help in easy identification of personal creams and lotions so they won't need labelling. Always keep creams in a wide-necked container for easy access. If the preparation is likely to affect the eyes remember to label.

herbs which are rich in silica, such as horsetail, can be taken as a tea. Use a block of beeswax to massage the nails, or almond oil if you prefer. For a nail bath, in which you soak your nails, make a strong infusion of horsetail, strain and allow to cool before using.

We are probably more aware of our hands than of any other part of our body. After all the work that is expected of them it is no wonder that they can become sore, cracked and ingrained with dirt. A simple way to remove dirt from under the nails if to make a paste of sugar and a little washing up liquid, mixing the sugar and liquid together in the palm of your hand. Add a little water to the paste and then work well into the nails by rubbing your hands together. Rinse in warm water and dry.

In the 18th century such recipes were often more complicated, but effective none the less. Here is an 18th-century recipe for a paste for cleansing dirty hands that you might like to try.

Take 100 g/4 oz of blanched almonds, beaten fine, into a quart [editor's note: 900 ml/ 2 pints] of milk. As soon as it begins to boil, take it off, and thicken it with a couple of Yolks of Eggs. Set it on the fire again, let it be continually stirring both before and after the eggs are put in. When you take it off the fire, add two more spoonfuls of Oil, and put up in a Gallipot [author's note: an earthenware pot from the Mediterranean] for use. A bit of this about the Bigness of a Walnut rubbed about the hands, the dirt will rub off, and it will render them very soft and smooth.

When you have used it, it will be proper to put on gloves. If one Person only be to use, half the quantity may suffice to be made at once, for it will not hold good above a Week.

Personally, I have two favourite herbs for making into hand creams. They are rosemary and marigold (calendula). The recipes are given here.

Herbal preparations for the eyes

Eye washes are considered to be the most soothing form of treatment for tired and sore eyes. But do be careful: do not make too strong an infusion, or depend on one treatment for too long. If you have more than just occasional soreness, you must consult an optician or your doctor. I was once told that rue, in spite of its effect on the skin, was a good eye strengthener. With recent research disclosing that rue has a phototoxic effect, it would be very unwise to use an infusion on your eyes, as exposure to the sun could then have devastating results.

Safe eye tonics are: elderflower, eyebright and clary sage. For sore eyes you can use a weak infusion of yarrow or chamomile. For sties, try tansy, or rub onion juice on the area, very carefully. Tea bags, cucumber and even potato peel can be used as pads on the eyelids while lying down in a shady room. These will soothe and clear tired eyes. For a more herbal remedy, you can moisten cotton wool pads with witch hazel.

Marigold hand cream

Take 28 g/1 oz of marigold petals and add 600 ml/1 pint of almond oil, or good quality sunflower oil, placed in a bain marie. Simmer gently for 2 hours. Strain off the oil and put into a saucepan. Over a gentle heat add one ounce of beeswax and stir in until well absorbed. Pour into clean jars or containers and after cooling, seal and label.

This is a very gentle skin cream that can be used on the face as well.

Rosemary hand cream

Assemble the following ingredients: 84 g/3 oz coconut butter, 84 g/3 oz lanolin, 56 g/2 oz ground rosemary (fresh) , 28 g/1 oz beeswax. Put them all together in a pan (not aluminium) and heat gently until a creamy texture is achieved. Pour into jars and wait to cool before sealing.

This doesn't look too attractive, but the scent is wonderful and after a heavy day's gardening it seems to refresh the skin. It is however, rather greasy.

Herbal preparations for the skin

A leaf of mint mirrors the translucent qualities of herb soaps. The commercial market has hundreds of wonderful varieties to choose from, and it is so good to know that herb soaps don't have to smell of seaweed to do you good. Fragrance is of the essence.

If, like Lady Wishfort in Congreve's play *The Way of the World*, you look like 'an old peeled wall', then at least be glad you don't feel the need to cover it with the sort of drastic action advocated in the 16th century. Our skin needs to be cleansed and fed, not poisoned and bleached. The use of mercury in the form of mercuric sulphide and soliman, as well as white lead, turned many a face, including Elizabeth I's, into a ravaged, pitted mess. Thankfully, herbal preparations have become widely used, and more sinister chemical applications outlawed. There are now numerous creams, oils and other products available on the market, many of them dispensing with cruel animal-testing techniques. Here is an old recipe for cucumber lotion.

Half a peck [editor's note: 8.810 litres/8 quarts dry] of quince blossoms put in a pan, covered with cold water and simmered gently for an hour. Cut two large cucumbers into very thin slices and then chop finely. Put into the saucepan with the quince blossom water and boil for five minutes. Stain through muslin, and, when quite cold pour into bottles and tie down. To use, smear the lotion on the face and leave for at least ten minutes before washing.

Herbs that will benefit normal skin are sage, lady's mantle, peppermint, fennel and juniper. For oily skin use chamomile, yarrow or parsley in a strong infusion mixed with egg white or buttermilk to make a face pack. You can even try oatmeal or yogurt to help clean out the pores. For dry skin use comfrey, salad burnet, marigold and borage. There are a number of books devoted entirely to cosmetic herb preperations; by experimenting with various recipes you will soon discover the herbs that suit you .

177

Aromatherapy

romatherapy is the nearest you will get to a herbal hug. If stress or pain is making your life uncomfortable then consider a visit to your nearest qualified aromatherapist and you could well be on the way to correcting the imbalance that your body is experiencing.

The ancient Egyptians were the first to tap into the power of essential oils. By collecting herbs and steeping them in animal fats left in the sun, they were able to use the resulting blend in a medicinal way. The Arab apothecaries perfected the art of distillation and scented oils, and perfumes began to be exported to Europe. In 1928 a French scientist called René Maurice Gattefossé, published a book describing the art of *aromathérapie* in treating skin conditions. From this, interest grew in the new treatment, and the steam distillation of essential oils was perfected. This is not to be experimented with at home however, as the process requires specialist equipment and should be left to the experts, who use only the best unadulterated herbs and produce pure concentrated oils.

The principle of aromatherapy is based on the effect of scent on the olfactory nerve which transmits to the brain immediately and positively. By choosing the right essential oil for the physical ailment or mental state of the patient, the aromatherapist can achieve a result instantly and determine the treatment accordingly. The olfactory memory is the longest memory we have, and scents and smells from our childhood can be recognised and conjure up images from our past. We then recognise the scents that made us feel secure and these memories help to relieve the mental stress of adult life.

Although the use of essential oils is becoming fashionable, it should be stressed that these aromatics should be treated with great respect. Each drop of essential oil contains an enormous amount of plant material. This is very strong magic indeed.

Massage involves more than just the administering of a healing oil. The very fact that another human being is touching you completes the holistic treatment. There is no emotional or sexual involvement. The detached professional, however, has a caring role to play, helping to create a stable atmosphere and offering a sympathetic ear to the patient's problems. Never un-

derestimate the power of touch. It is a lost art and one we badly need to rediscover. The essential oil – diluted in a base oil such as grape seed, which is light and odourles – is massaged into the skin and absorbed into the system. At the same time the olfactory nerve is stimulated and the brain is receptive to the healing effects of the fragrance.

For pure, basic aromatherapy you can put one or two drops of essential oil on a tissue placed against your body within your clothing, and the natural heat from your body will release the aroma.

Another method is to place up to five drops of essential oil into a bath. Remember to agitate the water well before immersing yourself, as the concentration of the oil can irritate your skin if you come into direct contact with it.

The most common reason for anyone to visit an aromatherapist is to help relieve stress and related problems such as depression and gastric disorders. The need for physical communication without complications is often very strong. But inhibition can present a considerable barrier. The relaxing qualities of aromatic essential oils can help to break down these inhibitions and the body and mind are then freed to assist in the re-balancing programme.

The following are some of the primary esssential oils and their virtues

LAVENDER A calming sedative for anxiety and stress, insomnia, impatience, irritability; externally for bites and stings. **Note:** This is one oil that can be used neat, but not on babies.

ROSEMARY The most stimulating of all essential oils, for aches and pains in muscles and joints, circulation, mental fatigue and poor memory.

GERAMIUM Balancing and cleansing properties, harmonising, PMS, hormone imbalance, anxiety.

FRANKINCENSE Rejuvenating, heals stubborn wounds, soothes rheumatic pain, comforting, revives the vital spirit; used to treat nightmares.

CHAMOMILE Roman chamomile (*Anthemis nobilis*). Most female helper of essential oils. For PMS, period pains, cholic, calming, anger irritation. **Note:** Roman chamomile has over 150 compounds.

CLARY SAGE A euphoric oil, emenagogue, for period pains, sore throats, and as an anti-depressant. **Caution:**

Only use in small amounts and avoid drinking alcohol, as this can produce drowsiness.

All these essential oils have the ability to be blended to produce a synergistic (more powerful) effect in some chronic conditions. Remember to follow the rule that 'less is more' and do not be tempted to overdose. Always consult a qualified aromatherapist before embarking on experimentation and if using essential oils for pregnancy.

The ration for blending is no more than 10 drops in total to 30 ml/6 tsp of carrier oil. Examples of successful blends are as follows:

LAVENDER With all of the primary essential oils which are listed here.

ROSEMARY Geranium, lavender.

GERANIUM Chamomile, lavender.

FRANKINCENSE Rosemary, lavender.

Lavender oil and lavender water are two of the most popular uses of this safe, healing herb. The calming, sedative effect of lavender is most evident in its scent, which transmits power immediately via the olfactory nerves, and acts on the brain to assist in alleviating the most common ills of modern living – stress and anxiety.

CHAMOMILE Clary sage, geranium, lavender.

CLARY SAGE Chamomile, geranium, lavender.

Aromatherapy is now becoming a much respected science, assisting in the world of modern medicine in a very positive way. By treating it with respect and acting responsibly, this holistic way of healing is likely to take its place alongside medical treatment for all stress related illnesses and aid relaxation, thus enabling doctors to further the quality of care for their patients. It can also offer a most enjoyable way towards self help and comfort in our everyday lives.

Drying and Storing Herbs

Thomas Hyll, in *The Proffitable Arte of Gardening* (1568), wrote: 'And nowe those herbes (for the use of medicine) oughte to be gathered, and cut up, when as they be in a manner come, unto their full growthe, and that before the coloure of the flowers beginne to chaunge, and the seedes somewhat appeare. And this also oughte to be done, in a cleare and warm daye, and that they have been moystened with some showers fallinge two or three days before, so that they ought not to be gathered when any raine moisture, or wet dewe is on them, nor being then drie parched with the heate of the Sunne, nor in a raynie, and cloudie daie: for any of these do hynder the keaping any tyme in their virtue. Also they ought to be gathered when they be full of juice and freshe, and that not the smaller or bigger are to be chosen, but the meaner, and suche besides whiche fall not to whythering. And onely the tender toppes, the leaves, the flowers, are to be gathered and dried in the shadowe, in a place open towarde the Southe, not being moyste, and defended from the duste, and smoke, and for the better defending and preserving of theim, to be putte up in bagges close bounde at the mouthe, and in boxes for that use.'

Below: Herbs with the best leaves and flowers have been collected for drying. **Opposite:** Herbs drying naturally, hung in small bunches.

Making Herb Oils

Basil Oil

25 g/5 tbsp basil
600 ml/1 pint/2 ½ cups virgin olive oil
coarse sea salt

Break up the basil leaves with your fingers. Do not worry about any black stains on your fingers, they soon fade. Put the leaves in a mortar, add the oil a little at a time and pound briefly. Pour into a wide-necked jar and add a little coarse sea salt. Seal the jar and leave for two weeks before using. Turn occasionally. This can be topped up from time to time with fresh olive oil.

Pizza Oil

This is a selection of bitter herbs, peppercorns, garlic and chillis. I was given this recipe in Provence where they love to use herbs in their oils to add piquancy to their dishes. This was used on pizza. You can add more peppercorns and chilli according to taste.

300 ml/½ pint virgin olive oil
2 sprigs Rosemary officinalis
4 or 5 sprigs of thyme and marjoram
2 cloves of garlic

10 peppercorns
10 juniper berries
6 dried red chillis

Wash the herbs and pat dry between paper kitchen towel. Peel the garlic and cut in half to allow it to go into the neck of your bottle.

Pour the olive oil into a bottle and insert the rosemary, followed by garlic, then thyme and marjoram (the golden marjoram looks particularly good). Drop in the black peppercorns and juniper berries, followed last of all by the chillis. You can, if you wish, fill the neck with red chillis. Top up with olive oil and cork the bottle. Leave for two weeks, turning occasionally, before using. This also can be topped up from time to time in order to keep the herbs covered in oil.

Opposite: Tarragon, basil and aromatic bitter herbs have been preserved in vinegar and olive oil. The oil can be 'topped up' as you use it in order to keep the herbs constantly covered. This is a very good way of ensuring you have fresh herbs over the winter months.

Nothing changes much in the world of gardening, except spelling perhaps. Thomas Hyll's advice on drying and harvesting have as much relevance today as they did four hundred years ago. The rules are simple. Always harvest on a dry day, preferably with at least two dry days beforehand. Do not pick until after the dew has dried on the leaves, and before the sun has warmed the plants too much. Always choose the best looking herbs, just before flowering, in the case of culinary herbs; or, if you want flowers, before they begin to go to seed. Above all, dry your herbs in an airy place away from sunlight. So much of this advice seems common sense, but it is so easy to forget, in the excitement of the moment, and then wonder why your jars contain grey dust instead of crisp dry leaves.

Methods of drying

Drying needs to be done as quickly as possible if the herbs are going to retain their quality. In some cases, as with artemisias or soft shrubby plants, you can tie them in loose bunches and hang them in a shady attic, or shed, as long as they have plenty of ventilation. Drying this way should take only one or two days. In the case of mints, lemon balm and soft-leafed herbs such as basil, then it helps to use an oven on a low heat, keeping the door open. Alternatively, you can even use the micro-wave. I don't possess a micro-wave oven so I can't recommend it personally, but I am told it can be quite effective. Place the leaves and shoots on a light baking tray with greaseproof paper under them, or on a cake rack, allowing air to circulate all around. Using an oven needs vigilance, as the time taken is quite swift compared to more natural methods.

If you are good at DIY you can make your own drying cupboard with tiered racks covered in stretched muslin or fine netting. If you have a shed you can develop this idea on a grander scale with shelves all around the walls, and an electric heater or small stove to assist the process. Do not forget the vital ventilation.

You may be tempted to dry your herbs in bunches in the kitchen. This gives a very pretty, decorative effect, but you will never lose all the moisture. The herbs also attract grease and dust, therefore they should not be stored in jars or containers as they will quickly disintegrate and go mouldy.

Opposite: A beautifully strong, container-grown mint that is absolutely ripe for harvesting so the leaves can be dried for winter. Mint needs to be dried as quickly as possible so that it will not become limp and black. It is quite disheartening to see how soon it can deteriorate. Keep some to hang in the kitchen, where it will deter flies.

Methods of storing

As soon as the herbs are dry, place them in dry, screw-top jars or bottles. Always keep them in a shady place, completely away from direct light. Should you see any signs of moisture appearing, then you must remove the leaves and thoroughly dry them again before replacing in a clean, dry jar.

Other ways of storing herbs include freezing and preserving in oil. Freezing works very well for basil and parsley. For many herbs, however, the freezing process seems to take away their vital flavour and reduces them to limp blandness when they are defrosted. Place the basil leaves directly into a small carton. There is no need to wash if you have grown your herbs organically, or to cut up the leaves. Seal the lid and place in the freezer. When you need a leaf, just remove and crumble into your dish without defrosting. Parsley also retains its flavour using this method.

The flowers of borage can be preserved by placing then in an ice cube tray and filling the compartments with water, then freezing. Not only do they preserve very well, but they also look extremely decorative when added to drinks.

To preserve herbs in olive oil, always use the virgin first pressings. The light green colour gives a very pleasing effect. Make sure the leaves you use are completely dry after washing them as otherwise mould can develop later on.

Herb Vinegar

Another method of storing herbs is to make herb vinegars. Use white-wine vinegars. Herbs that make good vinegars are: tarragon, dill, garlic and shallots.

Tarragon Vinegar

150 ml/10 tablespoons of tarragon   *600ml/1 pint of white wine vinegar*

Remove the tarragon leaves from the stems and place into a mortar. Pound briefly with your pestle. Heat 150ml/ 5 fl oz of vinegar to boiling point and pour slowly over the tarragon. Pound for a few moments and add the rest of the vinegar. Place a piece of muslin or kitchen towel over the mortar and allow to cool. When cool, pour the contents into a wide-necked jar and seal. Leave for two weeks and turn the jar upside-down occasionally. After two weeks strain the vinegar into a bottle and insert a cork. You can at this stage add a whole sprig of tarragon, washed and patted fry. This avoids the necessity of placing a large label on the bottle, which would spoil its appearance.

— Growing Herbs Organically —

The most important thing to remember about growing herbs is that you are often growing plants for human consumption. In this case the natural strength of the herb is an essential factor. All herbs can be grown naturally without the aid of chemical fertilisers. Many are introductions from the wild and are classed as indigenous. Those that have been introduced from abroad have been cultivated without relying on chemical feeds and pesticide.

In mass commercial cultivation it is necessary to use well controlled pesticides, but policing of the herb industry, particularly of responsible members of the British Herb Trade Association, is very rigid in its restrictions on the use of pesticides and fertilisers. Yet for the individual, small grower in their private plot or garden, there is no reason why an organic principle should not be adopted.

Your herb garden should be a safe haven for bees and other animals. The herbs are there to help you. You can make up safe, harmless pesticides and insect repellents. Having prepared the soil well in the initial stages, then add natural fertilisers made from comfrey, yarrow and nettle. Add a few leaves of comfrey and nettle to a bucket of water and cover for two weeks to create a rich liquid feed. Alternatively, you can do as I have done and place a string bag of fresh comfrey leaves in a water butt and strain off the water for a light feed of your vegetables throughout the growing season. Yarrow and nettle, as well as comfrey, can be added to your compost heap to activate it.

Making a compost heap

If you are fortunate enough to have an area of your garden where you can create a compost heap then there is no finer way of recycling household waste and garden material for feeding and improving your soil. This in turn helps strengthen the roots and root systems of your herb garden.

A great deal has been written about the creation of compost heaps, with the result that it appear to be daunting. Do not let this put you off: it's not that difficult. Foxes may come to have a chew over the raw and cooked remains of vegetable, but they play an advantageous role, as they are a deterrent to vermin.

The principle of compost making is to turn soft, waste plant material into rich humus as quickly as possible. A few rules must be followed:

• Enclose your compost heap in a well ventilated wooden or mesh structure. This helps the materials to heat up quickly and so break it down.
• Keep it slightly moist or cover with old sacking or carpet to retain moisture and heat.
• Only use soft material. Twigs and woody material will not break down quickly.
• Turn the compost frequently and do not be tempted to dump all your grass clippings on at one go. Put a few on at a time and add activators such as comfrey, nettle and yarrow.
• Build up your heap as quickly as possible, and then make another, for next year.
• With herbs the compost can be applied when not quite reduced to a friable state. This encourages earthworm activity.
• Woody material can be burned and the ashes added to the compost.

Opposite: Thick stems, as on this red valerian, do not break down as quickly as soft leaf and are best shredded before adding to the compost. **Above:** Comfrey is a most useful herb, providing food for the soil and helping to organically activate your compost heap. To use as a soil improver, put the leaves directly onto the soil in early autmn.

All compost heaps literally have a life of their own and can turn you into an obsessive compost maker. Give in to this a little. It's a great relaxer at the end of a hard day at the office.

Leaf mould is equally useful as a mulch. If you are able to acquire some from local woodland then do so. It takes at least two years to make your own in piles of autumn leaves enclosed by chicken wire. If you have the room it's very rewarding to your patience: if not, revert to well composted forest bark.

Since adopting an organic principle and allowing nature her sway I have been surprised to notice how many herbs seem to have a built-in immunity to pests and disease. No one can stand idly by and watch greenfly attack their roses. But companion planting, such as growing garlic and chives around roses, does seem to help the herbs gain in strength and so fend off the ravages of aphids.

Soap-based pesticides kill off greenfly, and ladybirds are not harmed as they hunt them too. Bees become more and more in number as they realise the power of natural cultivation. It can take a little time for your garden to adjust to its dependence on chemical products, which can, in the case of herbs, cause plants to grow on too quickly, so that they become soft and 'green', thereby weakening their defenses.

It is encouraging to realise that nature has her own way of aiding cultivation, so that the human hand can be employed elsewhere.

Hazardous Herbs

A report in the newspapers in June 1990, high-lighted the phototoxic effects of rue (*Ruta graveolens*) on the skin. The highly responsible article referred to a case where children playing with the flowers of plants in the garden on a hot, sunny day had broken out in painful blisters and brown stains. Doctors were baffled until the mother of one of the children took cuttings of the plants they had been play-ing with to the hospital. Now, some years on, there need be no more ignorance on the part of doctors re-garding hazardous plants, as the Royal Botanic Gardens at Kew have developed a system called PLATO (PLAnt TOxins – UK) which provides information at the press of a button on all poisonous and hazardous plants in the United Kingdom.

Before you go rushing out into your garden to tear out your rue, and any other hazardous plant, it is worth considering the true dangers of hazardous herbs. Certainly, not all herbs are 'safe': but very few are life threatening, and most of them are growing in the wild.

Responsible organisations such as the Herb Trade Association police the labelling of their plants, and herbs such as rue are clearly labelled at the retailers with warnings about the effects they may have on some people. The fact that rue does not affect all types of skin is valid. Just as medicinal herbs do not necessar-ily work in the same way for every individual, then so it is with hazardous plants. Poisonous plants, however, do affect everyone in exactly the same way – and they are dangerous.

If you are in the habit of picking wild berries, or making tisanes from wild plants, it is as well to identi-fy your plants very carefully. The umbelliferal family in particular is a minefield when it comes to poisons. Goutweed, wild angelica, hedge parsley, cow parsnip and sea carrot have a striking similarity to fools parsley, wild chervil, hemlock and hemlock water dropwort. These last four plants are extremely dangerous. The

Opposite: Henbane, *Hyoscyamus niger*, grows in sandy, waste places, very often near the sea. It is so toxic that its use in medicine is now severely restricted. The effect of henbane on the nervous system can be deadly. The fetid smell of this downy plant gives some indication of its poisonous nature.

Poisonous plants

Aconite	Hemlock water dropwort
Black bryony	Henbane
Buttercup	Ivy
Columbine	Laburnum
Baneberry	Meadow saffron
Deadly nightshade	Mistletoe
Fool's parsley	Spindle tree
Foxglove	White bryony
Dog's mercury	Black nightshade
Hemlock	Yew

great philosopher Socrates was put to death by being made to drink hemlock, so be warned.

Unless you choose to grow any of the above herbs in your garden then you have little to fear. And even if you do have buttercup, columbine, foxglove, ivy, laburnum and yew there is no harm in growing them as long as you are aware that eating any part of them in large quantities is potentially harmful. There has been only one recorded fatality from any of these in recent years, and that was from laburnum seeds.

Be aware and take precautions if you have children who are naturally curious about plants. Begin to educate them about which plants are harmful, and warn against eating any berries in the wild until they know exactly what they are. It would be a pity to deprive any child of the joy of blackberry picking.

The most common problems encountered in the garden are caused by skin contact with plants that cause allergic reactions. Common nettle rash, or, urticaria, is caused by a chemical reaction, as is the sting from

Opposite: The deadly nature of the laburnum, *Laburnum anagyroides,* is particularly evident in the seeds and pods. Seek medical help at once if there is any suspicion of ingestion. **Above:** Hemlock, *Conium maculatum,* is recognisable by the purple blotches on the stems. **Left:** Wild carrot, *Daucus carota sylvestris,* has a white root, as opposed to the orange root of the cultivated form. Unlike hemlock, it is quite safe.

stinging nettle, or from a specific immune response, such as a specific reaction to certain vegetables or fruit.

Rue is not the only culprit when it comes to blisters. Apparently, beggars used to rub their faces with buttercups to make themselves look sick, in the hope that people would take pity on them. The phototoxic effect is caused by the reaction of ultra-violet (UV) rays from the sun on the volatile oil secreted by the plant. A small number of umbelliferals including, of all things, parsley, parsnips and carrots, can have a phototoxic effect, but it is rarely severe. The invention of the strimmer has caused more problems with skin reactions than has been seen for some time. Because most men operating strimmers do so on a hot sunny day, they also are inclined to strip to the waist and so expose their torsos to a bombardment of plant material and sap, which, in the case of an umbelliferal such as cow parsley, causes a positive grapeshot effect on the skin. I have seen photographs of people who have been 'attacked' in this way and they are not a pretty sight. When using such machinery it is best to dress like a spaceman, however hot it may be.

Allergies are more likely to affect certain people, and the usual safeguards apply. If you experience an allergic reaction of any kind seek professional help immediately. Poison ivy can cause quite bad blistering and discomfort, although there is little evidence of it being widespread in this country. There have been, however, a number of recorded cases of skin reactions to this plant in the United States. Feverfew can cause contact dermatitis. The problem of mouth ulcers was mentioned earlier but at least that can be treated with tincture of myrrh.

Some of the worst cases of what might be termed herb abuse have been from the over-use of essential oils. I have read recently of two recorded fatalities in the United States from excessive use of pennyroyal essential oil in attempting home abortions. The need to use essential oils in moderation cannot be stressed enough. They are highly concentrated forms of herbal oil and are therefore extremely powerful.

Below: An example of the blistering caused by contact with rue, *Ruta graveloeus*, on a sunny day. The blistering could last for up to eight weeks, but will eventually fade. **Opposite:** Tansy, *Tanacetum vulgare*, has traditionally been associated with long life, but recent research has show that, in large doses, it can cause kidney and brain damage.

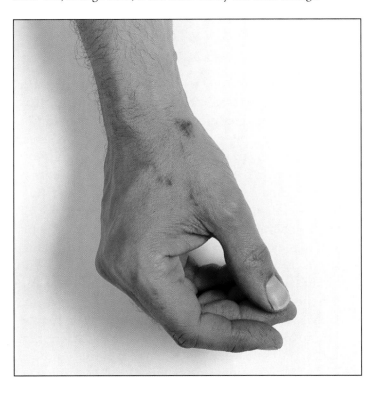

The use of herbs in pregnancy

Most doctors refrain from any medication, if possible, during pregnancy. Medical herbalists caution against some herbs, but are happy to suggest absolutely safe herbs such as chamomile, psyllium seed and dandelion, among others. However there are some herbs which in the normal state of events are safe, but can be dangerous in pregnancy. These are the herbs that bring on delayed menstruation and therefore become abortives. The most common, mentioned in this book are: marjoram, pennyroyal, rosemary, rue, sage, tansy, thyme and wormwood. There are others not mentioned here but they tend to be more specialised and so more likely to be prescribed by a medical herbalist who will not use them if ithere is any suggestion of pregnancy.

Do not panic over the culinary herbs used to flavour food. These will not be present in anything like the concentrations that can cause harm. Always consult a qualified member of the National Institute of Medical Herbalists, recognisable by the letters MNIMH or FNIMH after their name, or a doctor at the onset of pregnancy. This is not a time for self medication.

Cause for concern

In recent years a number of herbs have caused some concern among researchers: comfrey, male fern, mistletoe and sweet flag in particular. Although, in the case of comfrey, experiments have been conducted using large amounts of plant material, nevertheless, until further evidence is forthcoming it might be advisable to refrain from using comfrey as a tisane.

In spite of such precautions, your herb garden can still be a safe place; it is important to remember that the herbs mentioned here are merely classed as hazardous. Lists drawn up by well-meaning researchers include ornamental plants such as daffodils, tulips, nicotiana, hyacinth, and autumn crocus, and vegetables such as tomatoes and rhubarb. Without these in our gardens life would be pretty empty. Sensible people do not plant daffodil bulbs among the onions, nor do they include tulip heads in salad. When we are told that chives are hazardous because they make your eyes water then it will be time for the uprising. Until then, enjoy your herbs and don't put rue near the swimming pool or children's sandpit, and above all, teach your children the dangers as well as the pleasures of gardening.

Legends and Superstitions

At a time when there was no street lighting, when people went in fear of being 'elf-shot', when plague began to sweep through the land and death could strike quickly and at any moment, the following words, translated by Archbishop Cranmer during the reign of the sickly boy-king Edward VI, must have been comforting: 'Thou shalt not be afraid for any terror by night: nor for the arrow that flieth by day; /For the pestilence that walketh in darkness: nor for the sickness that destroyeth in the noon-day.' Psalm 91, *The Book of Common Prayer* (1549).

In pagan times herbs were recognised as a gift from the gods. There was a plant for all ills. Fear of the unknown, nurtured by superstition, made people believe that powerful outside forces determined their destiny. Only the white witches and cave hermits could make them better when sickness overtook them, using the secret power of plants, and unlocking their 'magic' with strange incantations.

The leech doctors, who were in direct opposition to the monastic orders, were concerned with 'elf-disease' being entirely concerned with being 'elf-shot'. In *The Leech Book of Bald* the famous Anglo-Saxon treatise on herbal medicine, there are incantations to banish elves. These are not the jolly-eye creatures of darkness who dipped their arrows in poisonous herbs and fired them at unsuspecting country folk. Dreams and nightmares were all attributable to elves and hobgoblins. The church took all of this on board and quickly set about converting the ignorant and superstitious to a protective, caring, loving doctrine, introducing all the characters of the Christian religion in new names for old plants, and imbuing them with Christian 'magic'.

It is not surprising when you see the perfectly spherical drops of dew on the leaf of lady's mantle, that this herb is particular was looked on as a 'magic' herb. The dew drops should be collected at dawn, when they are supposed to be most powerful. The leaves and flowers are used medicinally to promote pregnancy and assist in an easy birth.

So it is, that we now recognise plants such as lady's mantle, referring to Our Lady Mary, mother of Christ; St John's wort, a healing hypericum that produces an oil from its flowers that is the colour of blood, and supposedly represents the martyrdom of St John: and monkshood, known previously as wolfbane.

The most respected of all healing herbs, rosemary, became the subject of a delightful Christian legend. When Mary and Joseph fled to Egypt with the baby Jesus, they rested on the way by a rosemary bush, which provided shade from the heat of the sun. Mary placed her blue cloak over the bush, which was covered in pure white flowers. When the cloak was removed the flowers had turned to the soft blue of Mary's mantle.

Rosemary was reputed to flower at midnight on Twelfth Night. It was a symbol of constancy and deep friendship. It is supposed to grow to the height of a man, no taller than Christ was, and to live only as long as he; thirty-three years. If my first *R. officinalis* is anything to go by, then this is quite possible, although, sadly, it is no more, having succumbed to the bulldozer at my old allotments.

The passion flower, a recognised medicinal plant for insomnia and irritable bowel syndrome, was so called by the Jesuits soon after its discovery in North America. The Mexicans call it 'the flower of five wounds'. Symbolic of the Crucifixion, its triple style signifies the three nails of the cross (they do resemble old nails); the centre of the flower represents the column on which Christ was scourged; the filaments are the crown of thorns; the calyx resembles a halo and the leaf is the shape of a spear head (that was used to pierce Christ's side). The beautiful colour is said to be akin to heaven, and the life of the flower (just three days) symbolises the three days up to the resurrection.

Parsley, while succumbing to some monastic doctrine, is primarily a plant associated with evil. It was said that to pick parsley while reciting someone's name would guarantee their death within seven days. Parsley takes a long time to germinate because it goes to the devil and back seven times before doing so. It is therefore necessary to sow it on Good Friday to free it from the devil's grip. It brings bad luck if given away, but will grow well if stolen from another garden. It will only grow successfully if the mistress of the house is the one who wears the trousers, and it will not grow in the garden of a cuckold. I once told a customer this who thanked me profusely and said 'That explains everything,' and went away with a secret smile on her face.

If you give parsley away you give your good luck with it. If you are in love, try to avoid cutting parsley, or your love will die. Transplanting it invites disaster on the home to which it has gone.

For such a popular plant it is hard to understand why parsley has had such a bad press. True, it is difficult to grow, but there's no need to be so spiteful about it. Basil seems to have avoided the Church altogether and retained its mysterious mythology, associated with death and scorpions.

A pot of basil

In the tale of Isabella and the pot of basil, Boccacio tells of the murder of Isabella's lover by her jealous brothers, who hid the body in the woods. This tale is depicted in the painting *Isabell and the Pot of Basil* by Holman Hunt. Having discovered the body and retrieved the head, Isabella is shown standing protectively over a large china bowl which has basil growing out of the head of her beloved.

Salome is said to have used the same means to preserve the head of John the Baptist. This gave credence to the belief that basil thrives on the brains of a murdered man. Another early theory suggest that becasue scorpions shelter in its shade, basil can cause scorpions to grow inside the head. Nicholas Culpeper, after describing its strange qualities – in drawing out poison, its enmity to rue (a recognised antidote to poison) and its supposed aphrodisiac effects – then concludes: 'I dare write no more of it.'

In India, from where basil originates, the sacred basil, *Ocimum sanctum* is sacred to the Hindu god Vishnu, and a leaf is placed between the hands at funerals.

The vinegar of the four thieves

Plague swept through Europe in the 17th and 18th centuries with devastating loss of life. Two germicides, rue and wormwood, came into their own with various recipes concocted as protection against the pestilence. Many of these recipes found their origin in 'the vinegar of the four thieves'. Legend has it, that when the plague hit Marseilles in 1722, four villains were caught robbing houses of infected persons, and yet showed no sign of the disease themselves. They were brought before the French magistrates. In their testimony they confessed to making a herbal preparation which they

Yet mark'd I where the bolt of
   Cupid fell:
It fell upon a little western flower,
Before milk-white, now purple with
   love's wound,
And maidens call it, Love-in-idleness.
Fetch me that flower; the herb I sho'd
   thee once;
The juice of it on sleeping eyelids laid
Will make or man or woman
   madly dote
Upon the next live creature that it sees.

Oberon, *A Midsummer Night's
Dream*, William Shakespeare

drank and doused themselves with every two hours. With great wisdom the judges granted the men their freedom in return for the recipe. All recipes contain rosemary, sage, mint, lavender, rue and wormwood with garlic and sometimes cinnamon, nutmeg, cloves and camphor. A simple recipe from a Virginian housewife uses two quarts of apple cider vinegar and handfuls of lavender flowers, rosemary, sage, wormwood, rue, mint and garlic buds. This mixture would be left in the sun for two weeks and then strained off for use. Similar recipes are used today to fumigate sick rooms.

To illustrate the strength of the belief in this remedy: when, in 1760, a rumour spread that plague had broken out again, the price of rue and wormwood went up by 40 per cent at Covent Garden Market.

Rue has always been a powerful herb in the world of superstition. The Romans believed that it gave second sight, and priests wore it about their necks. Strangely, this continued into the Christian church with the use of rue as an aspergillum to anoint the congregation with Holy Water. Rue was considered to be a great protective herb against illness, as an antidote to poison, and to strengthen and control weapons of war. Arrowheads dipped in rue were supposed to find their mark, and grapeshot used to be boiled in rue water. John Gerard tells us that weasels would seek out rue to eat before attacking a snake. It has been used both to curse and to bless. The expression, 'to rue the day', still applies to retribution, having originated apparently in the county of Hertfordshire, when a rejected lover threw a bunch of rue at her former lover on his wedding day. The curse was rumoured to have been successful and the expression entered into our language.

Herbs associated with witchcraft

Elder leaves, rowan trees, mallow, rosemary, St John's wort and mugwort are all supposed to ward off witches. However, if you wish to see a witch then you would need to make a bag of herbs and wear it next to your heart. Favourite plants would be broom, rue, agrimony, and ground ivy. Witches were in existence in the folklore of ancient Rome and ancient Greece.

Opposite: A number of herbs are referred to in Shakespeare's plays for their magic qualities. Heartsease, or love-in-idleness, is one of the most beautiful and the most gentle of all the potions suggested, and was considered to be a prime ingredient in love potions.

They have always been associated with darkness and necromancy, inhabiting burial grounds where they would gather their wild herbs making potions and wicked charms. Although the most fashionable image is of a 'black, midnight hag', there were white and even grey witches. They were ruled over by the Greek goddess, Hecate, queen of Hades.

In Shakespeare's play *Macbeth* Hecate praises the witches for concocting an evil potion containing 'Root of hemlock, digg'd in the dark' together with 'slips of yew'. This conjures up various apparitions to foretell the future fate of the thane. All herbs associated with witches are of a poisonous or 'dark' nature. Yew is traditionally grown in the west side of churchyards because the sun's afternoon rays were considered to be the strongest, and the toxins from the dead bodies were thus drawn up through the roots and expelled into the air through the foliage. Herbs would be gathered under cover of darkness or from heavily shaded woodlands. Roots make up a large number of recipes. William Coles, in his *Art of Simpling* describes witches' herbs, and charms to protect against them:

The Oyntment that Witches use is reported to be made of the fat of Children digged out of their graves; of the juices of Smallage, Woolfsbaine and Cinquefoyle mingled with the meale of fine Wheat. But some suppose the soporiferous Medicines are likeliest to do it, which are Henbane, Hemlock, Mandrake, Nightshade, Tobacco, Opium, Saffron, Poplar Leaves & c. They take likewise the roots of Mandrake … and make thereof an ugly Image, by which they intend to exercise their Witchcraft… Those that are used against Witchcraft, are mistletoe which if one hang about the neck, the Witches can have no power of him. The roots of Angelica doe likewise availe much in the same case, if a man carry them about him, as Fuchsius saith.

Amulets were a favoured form of protection, worn about the neck in the same way people wear crucifixes today. The herb material, or, in some cases animal teeth, hares' feet and so on, would be accompanied by a paternoster and ritual verse. In O. Cockayne's book, *Leechdoms, Wortcunning and Starcraft of Early England*, published by Rolls Series, London 1864-66, he refers to a charm against the 'stitch': 'draw a Cross and sing three times this over the place with a Paternoster: Longinus, the soldier pierced our Lord with a lance and the blood stopped and the pain ceased'.

Key

A Annual	B Biennial	P Perennial	C Cuttings	D Root Division	HEAT Heated Greenhouse

HERB	PROPAGATION	LATE WINTER	SPRING	SUMMER	AUTUMN	EARLY WINTER	LIFE
Marigold	Sow seed (self seeds)		✔				A
Marjoram	Divide roots cuttings	✔ D	✔ C	✔ C			P
Meadowsweet	Sow seed divide roots		✔ D				P
Mint	Divide roots cuttings	✔ D	✔ D	✔ C			P
Myrtle	Take cuttings			✔ C			P
Nettle	Divide roots	✔	✔				P
Parsley	Sow seed	✔	✔	✔	✔	✔	B
Rose	Take cuttings			✔			P
Rosemary	Take cuttings		✔	✔	✔		P
Rue	Sow seed take cuttings			✔ C			P
Sage	Divide roots cuttings		✔	✔ C			P
St. John's Wort	Sow seeds divide roots		✔ D				P
Savory (Summer)	Sow seed		✔				A
Savory (Winter)	Cuttings		✔ D/C	✔	✔ D		P
Sorrel	Divide roots sow seed	✔ D	✔				P
Southernwood	Take cuttings		✔	✔ C	✔ C		P
Salad Burnet	Sow seeds		✔				P
Sweet Cicely	Sow seed divide roots		✔ D		✔ D		P
Tansy	Sow seed divide roots		✔ D				P
Tarragon (French)	Divide roots cuttings	✔	✔	✔	✔		P
Thyme	Divide roots cuttings sow seed	✔	✔	✔	✔		P
Wall Germander	Sow seed cuttings divide roots		✔	✔ C	✔ D		P
Woodruff	Divide roots			✔			P
Wormwood	Divide roots take cuttings		✔ D	✔ C			P
Yarrow	Sow seed divide roots		✔ D				P

MAINTENANCE CHART

HERB	SPRING	SUMMER	AUTUMN	WINTER	SITE	COMMENTS
Alpine Strawberry		Harvest ripe fruits		Light mulch	Semi-shade	
Angelica	(Late) Harvest	Cut back			Semi-shade	
Basil		Pinch back	Cut off flower heads	Bring indoors before frosts	Full sun	Water in midday sun
Bay	Feed if in containers	Prune and shape	Bring to shelter of house or indoors		Sunny	
Bergamot		Harvest for tisanes	Cut back dead growth	Light mulch	Sunny (Moist)	
Borage		Harvest for summer drinks	Cut back large leaves		Sun or semi-shade	
Catnip			Trim back lightly after flowering		Sun or semi-shade	
Chamomile	Feed 'Treneague'	Harvest and cut back flowers			Sunny	Only cut flowers from Anthemis nobilis
Chervil	Harvest all year round				Light shade	
Chives	Regular cutting Remove flower heads if using for cooking			Dies down	Light shade	Makes good border if flowering
Comfrey		Cut back on a regular basis		Use leaves as soil dressing	Light shade	
Coriander		Harvest continually			Full sun	Successional seed sowing in summer
Costmary		Remove flower heads for strong leaf growth			Full sun	
Cotton Lavender	Late spring clip to shape	Clip hedging to stop flowering	Remove flower stems		Full sun	
Dill		Harvest			Sunny	
Evening Primrose			Cut back and scatter seeds			
Fennel		Harvest leaves	Harvest seeds		Sunny	
Feverfew	Check for self seeders	Keep a watch for aphids			Sunny	
Foxglove				Leaf mould mulch	Sun or light shade	Keep apart from comfrey
Good King Henry		Cut leaves regularly	Remove flower heads		Sun or light shade	
Hyssop	Cut back to new growth		Remove flower heads for drying		Full sun	
Lady's Mantle		Harvest flowers for decoration			Sun or light shade	Flowers and leaves for tisane
Lavender	Trim to shape		Remove flower stalks		Full sun	
Lemon Balm	Cut back to ground	Cut back mid summer	Remove dead growth		Sunny	
Lemon Verbena	Plant out after frosts	Trim back late summer	Light mulch if being left out	Bring in for winter	Full sun	
Lovage		Harvest on regular basis and remove flower heads to encourage leaf			Sunny	Good flower decoration herb

HERB	SPRING	SUMMER	AUTUMN	WINTER	SITE	COMMENTS
Marigold		Harvest flowers for salads			Full sun	
Marjoram	Cut back to new growth	Harvest	Cut flowers for drying		Full sun	
Meadowsweet		Harvest flowers	Cut back dead stems		Sun or light shade	
Mint		Keep in check by cutting low Do not cut back too hard			Sun or light shade	
Myrtle		Late summer training on wall			Full sun	
Nettle	Harvest young green tops	Keep in check by cutting back		Cut back hard	Sun or light shade	
Parsley	Begin to harvest	Feed well and harvest		Bring some in to overwinter	Sun and some shade	
Rose	Do not prune gallicas. Feed	Dead head flowers	Feed and trim back		Full sun	Light feed of manure in spring
Rosemary	Begin to harvest	Harvest	Harvest	Light harvest	Sunny	Can be cut all year
Rue	Cut back to new growth		Cut off flower heads		Full sun	Avoid cutting in full sun
Sage	Cut back late spring to new growth	Harvest leaves	Light mulch		Full sun	Tips can be removed early
St. John's Wort		Harvest flowers for oil	Cut back dead items		Sun or light shade	
Savory (Summer)		Harvest	Dies down		Full sun	Annual
Savory (Winter)	Cut back hard to new growth	Harvest	Harvest		Full sun	Perennial
Sorrel	Cut off flower heads as they appear for more leaf				Light shade	
Southernwood	Cut back to new growth	Remove flower heads			Full sun	
Salad Burnet		Cut off flower heads to encourage leaf growth		Harvest leaves	Sun or light shade	Produces leaf all winter
Sweet Cicely		Harvest			Sunny	
Tansy	Check for aphid	Harvest	Harvest for drying	Cut back dead stems	Sunny	
Tarragon	Watch for re-emergence	Harvest	Light mulch or bring indoors		Full sun	
Thyme	Light trim after flowering	Harvest and trim	Trim back lightly		Full sun	
Wall Germander	Clip to shape and cut back	Remove flower heads if hedge	Light trim		Sunny	
Woodruff	Cut off old growth early	Harvest for drying		Dies back	Light shade	
Wormwood	Check for aphid		Harvest for drying		Sun or light shade	
Yarrow		Harvest for compost heap as activator			Sunny	

HERB CLASSIFICATION

MINT FAMILY, *LABIATAE*

Typically square stems with simple leaves and two-lipped flowers in whorls among the leaves
Balm, *Melissa officinalis*
Basil, *Ocimum basilicum*
Catnip, *Nepeta cataria*
Hyssop, *Hyssopus officinalis*
Lavender, *Lavandula*
Marjoram, *Origanum*
Mints, *Mentha*
Oregano, *Origanum vulgare*
Pennyroyal, *Mentha pulegium*
Rosemary, *Rosmarinus officinalis*
Sage, *Salvia officinalis*
Savory, summer, *Satureia hortensis*
Savory, winter, *Satureia montana*
Thyme, *Thymus vulgaris*

CARROT OR PARSLEY FAMILY, *UMBELLIFERAE*

Umbelliferae have cylindrical stems, usually hollow with flat-topped flowers in clusters or umbels
Angelica, *Angelica archangelica*
Anise, *Pimpinella anisum*
Caraway, *Carum carvi*
Dill, *Anethum graveolens*
Fennel, *Foeniculum vulgare*
Parsley, *Petroselinum hortense*

DAISY FAMILY, *COMPOSITAE*

Composite have ray- or disc-shaped flowers like daisies
Chamomile, *Anthemis nobilis/Matricaria chamomila*
Cotton lavender, *Santolina chamaecyparissus*
Marigold, *Calendula officinalis*
Southernwood, *Artemisia abrotanum*
Tarragon, *Artemisia dracunculus*
Wormwood, *Artemisia absinthum*

HERBS FOR SUN AND SHADE

Herbs that grow well in full sun

Basil
Bergamot (needs moist soil)
Borage
Chamomile
Coltsfoot
Cotton lavender (*santolina*)
Dill
Fennel
Hyssop
Lavender
Lady's mantle
Lemon verbena
Marigold (*calendula*)
Marjoram
Rue
Sage
Salad Burnet
Southernwood
Summer and winter savory
Tarragon
Thyme

~

Herbs that grow well in heavy shade

Deadly nightshade
Lily of the valley
Woodruff

~

Herbs that grow well in partial shade

Angelica
Jacob's ladder
Lady's mantle
Lungwort

Pennyroyal
Valerian
Wood sage

~

Herbs that grow well in some shade

Chives
Comfrey
Foxglove
Honeysuckle
Lady's bedstraw
Lemon balm
Mint
Parsley
Purslane
St John's wort

~

HERBS CLASSIFIED BY HEIGHT

Low-growing herbs: up to 30 cm/12 in

Chamomile
Chives
Coriander
Marigold (*calendula*)
Parsley
Pennyroyal
Sage
Salad Burnet
Summer savory
Thyme
Winter savory

~

Medium-growing herbs: up to 90 cm /36 in

Basil
Bergamot
Borage
Chervil
Cotton lavender
Curry plant
Hyssop
Lavender
Lemon balm
Mints
Oregano
Rue
Southernwood
Tarragon
Wormwood

~

Tall-growing herbs: 90 cm/36 in and more

Angelica
Bay
Dill
Elecampane
Fennel
Hop
Lovage
Meadowsweet
Mullein
Rosemary
Witch hazel
Woad

~

HERBS FOR COLOUR

Red
Apothecary Rose
Bergamot
Clove pink
Pineapple sage

Blue
Borage
Flax
Jacob's ladder
Rosemary
Woad

Pink
Chives
Foxglove
Marjoram
Thyme 'Pink Chintz'
Thyme 'Annie Hall'
Wall Germander

Yellow
Elecampane
Evening Primrose
St John's wort
Sunflower
Tansy

Purple
Basil 'Dark Opal'
Foxglove
Red orach
Red sage (leaf)
Thyme

Green/yellow
Dill
Fennel
Lady's bedstraw
Lady's mantle
Lovage
Rue

Blue/purple & mauve
Catnip
Comfrey
Hyssop
Lavender
Lungwort
Thyme (common)

Orange
Nasturtium
Pot Marigold

White/cream
Double-flowered chamomile
Feverfew
Garlic chives
Lily of the valley
Thyme 'Albus'
Valerian
Woodruff

Variegated foliage

Ginger mint
Pelargonium 'Lady Plymouth'
Sage 'Icterina'
Sage 'Tricolour'
Thyme 'Doone Valley'
Thyme 'Gold stream'
Variegated apple mint
Variegated lemon balm

Silver/grey

clove pink
Costmary (alecost)
Curry plant
Lavenders
Santolina
Thyme 'Silver Posy'
Wormwood

USEFUL ADDRESSES

THE UNITED KINGDOM

Associations and Societies

British Herbal Medicine Association,
Lane House,
Cowling,
Keighley,
West Yorkshire BD22 0LX

British Herb Society,
134 Buckingham Palace Road,
London SW1W 9SA

British Herb Trade Association,
NFU Building,
22 Long Acre,
Covent Garden,
London WC2E 9LY

Chelsea Physic Garden,
Friends of the Chelsea Physic Garden,
66 Royal Hospital Road,
London SW3 4HS

Henry Doubleday Research Association,
Ryton Gardens,
Bryton-on-Dunsmore,
Coventry CV8 3LG

National Institute of Medical Herbalists,
148 Forest Road,
Tunbridge Wells,
Kent TN2 5EY

The Soil Association,
86 Colston Street,
Bristol BS1 5BB

The Tradescant Trust,
Friends of the Museum of Garden History,
Lambeth Palace Road,
London SE1 7LB

Herb Nurseries

Cheshire Herbs,
Fourfields,
Forest Road,
Little Budworth,
near Tarpoley,
Cheshire CW6 9ES

Hollington Nurseries,
Woolton Hill,
Newbury,
Berkshire RG15 9XT

Langley Boxwood Nursery,
National Collection - Buxus,
Rake,
near Liss,
Hampshire GU33 7JL

Jekka's Herb Farm,
Rose Cottage,
Shellards Lane,
Alveston,
Bristol BS12 2SY

Norfolk Lavender,
Henry Head,
Caley Mill,
Heacham,
Norfolk PE31 7JE

Seed Merchants

John Cambers Wild Flower Seeds,
15 Westleight Road,
Barton Seagrave,
Kettering,
Northamptonshire NN15 5AJ

CN Seeds – Wholesale,
Denmark House,
Pymoor,
Ely,
Cambridgeshire CB6 2EG

Dried Herbs and Herb Products

Hambledon Herbs,
Court Farm,
Milverton,
Somerset TA4 1NF

Neal's Yard Remedies,
14-15 Neal's Yard,
Covent Garden,
London WC2 9DP

Suppliers of Cut Herbs

R & G Stevens,
Lucas Green Nurseries,
Lucas Green Road,
West End,
Woking,
Surrey GU24 9LY

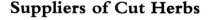

Herb Garden Design

Gardiners Herbs,
Anthony Gardiner,
35 Victoria Road,
Mortlake,
London SW14 8EX

Hollington Nurseries,
Simon Hollington,
Woolton Hill,
Newbury,
Berkshire RG15 9XT

Aromatherapy Oils and Supplies

Culpeper Ltd,
21 Bruton Street,
London W1X 7DA

The Dr Edward Bach Centre

Bach Flower Remedies,
Mount Vernon,
Sotwell,
Wallingford,
Oxon OX10 0PZ

~

Garden Furniture

Julian Chichester Designs,
(Furniture in Wood),
Unit 11,
33 Parson's Green Lane,
London SW6 4HH

Kate Viner,
(Metal Design),
97 Engadine Street,
London SW18 5DU

~

Statuary and Pots

Drummonds of Bramley,
Birtley Farm,
Horsham Road,
Bramley,
Guildford GU5 0LA

Whichford Pottery,
Whichford,
Shipston-on-Stour,
Warwickshire CV36 5PG

AUSTRALIA

Associations and Societies

Australian Herb Society,
PO Box 110,
Mapleton,
Queensland 4560

Henry Doubleday Research Association of Australia Inc,
816 Comleroy Road,
Kurrajong,
NSW 2758

Permaculture International,
PO Box 7185,
Lismorse Heights,
NSW 2480

~

UNITED STATES

Associations and Societies

Herb Society of America Inc,
9019 Kirtland,
Chardon Road,
Kirtland,
Ohio 44094

~

NEW ZEALAND

Associations and Societies

Herb Federation of New Zealand
PO Box 4055
Nelson South

ACKNOWLEDGEMENTS

The publisher and author would like to extend a special thanks to the following for their help and advice during the preparation of the book

Gardens: Mary Berry; Lambeth Palace; The Museum of Garden History, Lambeth; Warren and Jenny Prestwich; Jim and Lyn Boulden; Jan and Colin Ross-Munro and Jean-Luc; Simon and Judith Hopkinson; Raymond Notley; Marion Ganjou; Leeds Castle
Recipes: Mary Berry (page 140); Anna Del Conte (page 136); Liz and Dan Fleming (page 141); Jane Gardiner (pages 132, 134); Sarah Mertens (page 134)
Consultants: Christopher Hedley (Medical herbalist); Joanna Drew IFA ITEC (Aromatherapist)

Grateful thanks are also due to the following: Michael Billing; Mary Hearn; Paul Hunnings (The Barn Books, Penn, Buckinghamshire); Faber & Faber Ltd. for allowing the use of the quotation from Margery Fish and The Literary Trustees of Walter de la Mare and The Society of Authors for allowing the use of the quotation from Walter de la Mare.

The author would like to thank in particular Casey Horton for her invaluable help and unfailing support in the making of this book, and Jane, for her faith and patience and all the hard work she has done for him since he began his business.

INDEX